Person to Person Ministry

Soul Care
in the
Body of Christ

Martin and Deidre Bobgan

Scripture quotations are taken from the
Authorized King James Version of the Bible

Person to Person Ministry
Soul Care in the Body of Christ

Copyright © 2009 Martin and Deidre Bobgan
Published by EastGate Publishers
4137 Primavera Road
Santa Barbara, CA 93110

Library of Congress Control Number 2009902377
ISBN 978-0941717-21-2

Printed in the United States of America

Thus saith the LORD, Stand ye in the ways, and see, and ask for the old paths, where is the good way, and walk therein, and ye shall find rest for your souls.

Jeremiah 6:16

Study to show thyself approved unto God, a workman that needeth not to be ashamed, rightly dividing the word of truth. But shun profane and vain babblings: for they will increase unto more ungodliness.

2 Timothy 2:15-16

For a sample copy of *PsychoHeresy Awareness Letter*,
a free bimonthly newsletter about the intrusion of
psychological counseling theories and therapies
into the church, please write to:

PsychoHeresy Awareness Ministries
4137 Primavera Road
Santa Barbara, CA 93110

or call:

1-800-216-4696

www.psychoheresy-aware.org

Table of Contents

PART TWO: WHAT TO AVOID

Problem-Centered "Biblical" Counseling

What This Book Is All About

This book is about a Christ-centered approach to nurture the spiritual life of believers and to equip believers to fight the good fight of faith and thereby confront problems of living through exercising faith in Christ and the Word. **This book also reveals the innate sinfulness of problem-centered counseling, shows how problem-centered counseling leads Christians into feeding the flesh and quenching the Spirit, and gives reasons why Christians must abandon the problem-centered approach.**

When we say "problems," we are referring to problems normally taken to a psychotherapist or a biblical counselor. These are the personal, marital, and family problems that are discussed in seeking a resolution. **By "problems of living" we mean trials, tribulations, afflictions, and sufferings. While the expression "problems of living" is not in the Bible, we are purposely using this designation to explain what NOT to do.**

Person-to-person ministry must be Christ-centered rather than problem-centered. To meet this goal, we explain how both the one who ministers and the one who is receiving ministry will be doing three things: **(1) abandoning problem-centeredness; (2) embracing the biblical truth about the role of problems; (3) becoming Christ-centered on a daily basis.** The believer who remembers these three elements while ministering to fellow believers will find that, as fellow believers learn to give primary attention to Christ instead of talking about their problems, consider problems of living as opportunities for spiritual growth, and develop a

11

daily devotional life wherein they learn to walk according to the Spirit, the Lord will give them wisdom for the problems of living.

A basic premise of this book regarding such problems of living is that trials are attacks on the Christian's faith. They test the believer's faith and provide an opportunity to grow spiritually and to glorify God, who has given Christians all they need to confront such trials (Eph. 6:10-18; 2 Peter 1:3-4). Therefore how Christians view and respond to problems is extremely important. Those who draw alongside to minister should do so with the understanding that the person's faith is being challenged. There should be much sympathy because all believers have times when their faith is attacked. Therefore, they will not simply say, "You need more faith." They will recognize that the person is in the midst of spiritual warfare and needs encouragement in his walk with the Lord and spiritual support in holding up the shield of faith and wielding the sword of the Spirit, which is the Word of God (Eph. 6:10-18).

The Bible has much to say about trials, temptations, afflictions, and sufferings, or what we generally call "problems of living." Christians are not immune to problems. In fact, Christians should expect trials and various forms of suffering, including the kinds of problems of living that both psychological and biblical counseling address. Whether the problems are due to a believer's strong stand for the faith or an aspect of God's fatherly discipline or simply because we all live in a sinful world, every problem is a challenge to a believer's faith. Some are obvious attacks, but others are trials that bring a temptation to turn away from God or attempt to solve things apart from His involvement, His Word, and His will. Thus trials may tempt believers to lose patience and not trust God to work through the pain and suffering. Trials also tempt believers to sin against God for the sake of getting rid of unpleasant circumstances.

The Bible presents a view of problems of living very different from the usual human perspective. God uses such problems for His purposes, which include drawing people to Himself, conforming believers to the image of Christ, and building His Kingdom, all to His glory. God thus uses problems for His glory and our good. In contrast, ever since the counseling rage began, Christians have been using the Bible and God, often in combination with the wisdom of man, to solve and get past their problems. The means and the goal are diametrically opposed. God uses problems for our spiritual and eternal good, but in much Christian counseling people often attempt to use God and His Word primarily for elimination of and temporal relief from problems.

Utilitarian Christianity is not limited to seeker-sensitive churches, but pervades Christian counseling and much of what is called biblical counseling. Think about the contrast between God using trials for His purposes and people using God for theirs. One glorifies God and spiritually matures believers; the other dishonors God by using Him for personal gain (personal happiness, relief from problems, etc.). Does this mean that God's dear children are not to turn to Him and His Word in the midst of trials and seek His help? No! He is our Father. He has instructed us to call on Him, and He has promised to instruct and deliver us. However, there is a subtle but stark difference that can occur when the believer's goal is different from God's goal.

Early believers saw trials as God's gracious fatherly means of maturing His children in the faith. Rather than focusing on ways to solve the problems as the means of finding peace and happiness, the early Christians saw problems as opportunities for growing in faith and glorifying God. James urged believers to "**count it all joy when ye fall**

into divers temptations" (James 1:2) and to recognize that every trial is a test of faith and a call to spiritual arms. Thus they had a different perspective and a different "solution," so to speak.

If any group of believers suffered from problems of living, the early Christians did, to the point of great affliction, persecution, and martyrdom. Moreover, many of them had suffered horrendous childhoods, including slavery and all forms of abuse. The "talking cure" would never have sufficed any more than Job's counselors' "talking cure" of arrogance and condemnation. No, the early Christians needed more than that. They needed encouragement in their walk of faith. They needed to learn to use the shield of faith, the sword of the spirit, prayer, and the rest of the godly armor supplied with their new life in Christ. They needed their branches to be pruned with affliction so that the fruit of the Spirit would flourish.

They needed to learn the ways of the Lord and to encourage each other in the truths they had learned. They needed to remember and remind one another about the usefulness of trials, afflictions, and tribulation and how these can produce patience in trials, experience with God, hope in His promises, and the very love for God being shed abroad in their hearts by the Holy Spirit (Romans 5:3-5). They needed to hang on to the Lord with endurance and to come alongside the weaker one to help that person do so as well (Gal. 6:1-2). They needed to seek God for wisdom, believing that He would show the way (James 1:5-6). And through all of this they learned that James was right when he said:

> My brethren, count it all joy when ye fall into divers temptations; knowing this, that the trying of your faith worketh patience. But let patience have her perfect

work, that ye may be perfect and entire, wanting nothing (James 1:2-4).

The early believers came to experience the consolation of the Lord so that they could console one another along the arduous walk of faith in those days that were far more trying than today. Have we been deceived into the problem-centered talking cure when there is so much more to be gained through following the teachings of Scripture regarding trials, their source, their purpose, and their tremendous usefulness?

Years ago we were part of the biblical counseling movement (BCM). We spoke at conferences, promoted various BCM organizations, and wrote in support of biblical counseling. For reasons mentioned in this book and in our other writings, we left the BCM and became critics of it. One of the many reasons we left is because we realized that the very terminology (i.e., *counselor, counselee, counseling*) used in the movement was unbiblical. Primarily, we recognized that those in the BCM used a problem-centered approach similar to the psychological counseling movement that preceded it, while we used a Christ-centered ministry approach. We also realized that the training programs with their manuals, certificates, and degrees were intimidations to those individuals who should have been encouraged to minister without such obstacles to service.

It is our desire that, by reading this book, those who are maturing in the faith through the trials of life and walking daily in the faith will be encouraged to minister the care of souls to fellow believers. To accomplish this goal we have three parts to this book. In Part One we discuss **"What Not to Do"** by revealing the unbiblical shortcomings of the BCM as a contrast to true biblical ministry. Knowing **"What Not to Do"** can often be as important as knowing **"What Can Be Done."** In Part Two we discuss **"What to Avoid."** We recommend that one not become enmeshed in any system of counseling. **We demonstrate how what is called "biblical counseling" is problem-centered and inevitably leads to evil speaking[1] and should be avoided by all believers.** As examples we critique the nouthetic counseling approach developed by Dr. Jay Adams and promoted by the National Association of Nouthetic Counselors (NANC) and the inner-workings-of-the-heart approach espoused by Dr. David Powlison and promoted by the Christian Counseling and Educational Foundation (CCEF). Part Three is titled **"What Can Be Done."** In it we discuss what can be done to minister to those with problems of living. This is meant to be an encouragement to those who desire to minister and for those who are already doing so.

This book is **not** written to train Christians to become biblical counselors. The purpose of this book is to encourage those in the church who are called and gifted by God to minister Christ to other believers as needs and opportunities arise. There are numerous believers who are already prepared and equipped by God to minister to fellow believers who are facing trials and suffering from problems of living. God has prepared and equipped His children through His gifts of salvation, new life in Christ, the indwelling Holy Spirit, and His Word. He continues to prepare and equip them as they continue in His Word, walking according to their new life and maturing in the faith as they encounter various trials and life experiences.

We pray that more and more of those whom God has already prepared through His Word, the work of the Holy Spirit in their lives, and the fellowship of the saints will step out in faith to minister to one another in the Body of Christ as a result of reading this book.

PART ONE

What Not to Do

The Biblical Counseling Movement: God's Way or Man's Way?

1. Review

We have documented the faults of psychological counseling and enumerated the errors of the biblical counseling movement in our books and articles.[1] While we raise our concerns, we are not saying that there is nothing good in the psychological counseling movement or in the biblical counseling movement. Some psychotherapists may give some good advice in carnal areas and some biblical counselors function biblically. However, both movements intimidate believers from ministering to one another in the Body of Christ. **Both movements are problem-centered**, and there are enough individual and common faults in both movements to reject them.

In our book *Christ-Centered Ministry versus Problem-Centered Counseling (CCM)* we describe Christ-centered ministry and contrast it with problem-centered counseling. In *CCM* and other books we have written, we tell why Christians should **not** trust psychotherapy and the psychological counseling movement and also why Christians should **not**

17

trust the biblical counseling movement. We began *CCM* with the following radical proposal:

> **The radical proposal is to discourage problem-centered counseling and to encourage Christ-centered ministry, to overthrow intimidation from the psychological and biblical counseling movements, and thereby to free believers in local congregations to minister to fellow believers without psychological or biblical counseling manuals, workshops, seminars, degrees, or certificates.**[2]

In it we state the following purpose:

> **The purpose of this book is to reveal the origins and faults of problem-centered counseling, to describe Christ-centered ministry and how it differs from problem-centered counseling, and to encourage local congregations to minister as God has called them to do without the influence of the psychological or biblical counseling movements.**[3]

In order to explain Christ-centered ministry we begin by referring to the biblical counseling movement (BCM) and the errors committed by those involved. The biblical counseling movement is not that old. It started with Dr. Jay E. Adams' book *Competent to Counsel* in 1970. In it Adams developed a methodology of counseling. He later wrote:

> Over the past 12 years I have worked assiduously to produce a body of literature in a field that, prior to that time, **virtually did not exist**: the field of biblical counseling (bold added).[4]

Since the time Adams began the BCM it has grown phenomenally. We will give a number of reasons why we left the movement with the understanding that not all of the reasons apply to all of the biblical counselors. However, our conclusion is that not many who call themselves "biblical counselors" are truly biblical. One of the first issues we encountered was the similarity between the biblical counseling movement and the psychological counseling movement that preceded it. Many in the BCM have mimicked much of what is in the psychological counseling movement, **particularly its problem-centered format**.

Onerous Ones

We have often referred to the "Onerous Ones," which many in the biblical counseling movement use and which are similar to what happens in the psychological counseling movement. We discuss the details of the Onerous Ones in our book *Against "Biblical Counseling": For the Bible*.[5] Many in the biblical counseling movement have regular offices and follow these onerous ones: one-to-one (most of the time there is one counselor and one counselee, except in marriage counseling); one day a week (while this is the standard, some counselors meet more often with their counselees); one hour (the 50-minute hour is the standard); one week after another (for some it goes on weekly month after month and even year after year); one fixed price (many charge or encourage a donation for biblical counseling); one right after another (counselees often follow other counselees in the counseling lineup); one up/one down (the counselor is up as the expert and therefore the counselee is down). **There is no biblical precedence for this!** Those who function in this way are merely following those in the psychological counseling movement. In fact, if the psychological counseling movement did not exist, the biblical counseling movement would not have followed in its footsteps in the vocabulary and format in which it currently exists.

No Criticism within the Biblical Counseling Movement

Many biblical counselors have personally expressed agreement with one or more of our criticisms and especially with our position against charging fees for biblical counseling and against having separated-from-the-church biblical counseling centers. Nevertheless, they do not speak out. There is no outcry in opposition to these sinful practices even by biblical counselors who oppose them and especially no outcry by the leaders of the biblical counseling movement. There may be a brief mention of one or more of these sinful practices but nothing close to a protest about them. We have never heard or read any protest regarding a sinful practice connected to a name and/or organization in violation.

There seems to be an unspoken agreement that biblical counselors are not to be critical of sinful practices within the movement. This is a sure sign of how weak the biblical counseling movement truly is. We challenge leaders in the biblical counseling movement to openly criticize practices and teachings of the movement, provide the names of biblical counselors and/or organizations that are in error, and document those errors.

It is strange that there is such a reluctance to name names of those in the biblical counseling movement who are involved in unbiblical practices when Adams, who fathered the movement, wrote the following in his endorsement for our book *PsychoHeresy: The Psychological Seduction of Christianity*, defending us for doing so:

> Some people will say the Bobgans are hitting too hard—naming names and all that—but I don't think so. Whenever someone writes for the Christian public he sets forth his views to the scrutiny of others, but if others think what he says is dangerous to the church

they, like Paul (who named names too), have an obligation to say so.[6]

This same standard should be applied to the biblical counseling movement.

Unbiblical Nature of the Biblical Counseling Movement (BCM)

In the following sections we reveal the unbiblical nature of much of biblical counseling and what should be done in its place for sound biblical ministry. Not all of the unbiblical ideas and practices that we list are taught and practiced by all of the biblical counselors. However, after being thoroughly involved in the movement, having spoken at and conducted workshops for biblical counseling organizations, and having read and interacted with numerous biblical counselors, our conclusion is that NOT many who call themselves "biblical counselors" are truly biblical. The reason for the following discussion is to warn those who minister about **What Not to Do** and especially to encourage those who truly desire to minister to do it biblically.

2. Problem-Centered Counseling

When we use the word *problem*, **we are referring to those problems normally talked about with a psychotherapist or a biblical counselor.** They are the mental-emotional-behavioral problems for which people seek counseling help. **In speaking about the practices of the biblical counseling movement, we use the terms** *counselor*, *counselee*, **and** *counseling* **because it is their terminology.**

Problem-Centered Counseling and Sinful Communication

Problem-centered counseling inevitably leads to sinful communication. If one "listens in" to problem-centered biblical counseling communication, one will hear many violations of numerous Bible verses warning against such talk. These violations would include gossip, slander, and all forms of evil speaking about others. In Ephesians 4:31 Paul warns believers against evil speaking or blasphemy, which in the New Testament would include any communication that would devalue another person, as well as its more specific meaning of blaspheming God. Paul uses the Greek equivalent in reference to himself being evil spoken of in 1 Corinthians 10:30. Such speech is not edifying and is harmful to one another.

Other verses would bring up various negative and critical words with respect to such evil speaking. However, we choose to use the one word *sinful*, since that is what such communication amounts to. Because people spend so much time talking negatively about others during problem-centered biblical counseling, it is by its very nature a sinful way of trying to assist those with problems of living.

In the balance of Part One we give many reasons for our later conclusion that **"The biblical counseling movement as it currently exists must die."** We demonstrate that it is often appropriate to use the word *sinful* when referring to problem-centered biblical counseling conversations. In Part Two, "What to Avoid," we give two examples from two well-known biblical counseling approaches to reveal what normally goes on in what is called "biblical counseling." We discuss the problem-centered conversations as presented by these two approaches to show how sinful they are and why the biblical counseling movement needs to die. In Part three we tell "What Can Be Done."

Problem-Centered Counseling versus Christ-Centered Ministry

In problem-centered counseling, the Bible verses used are generally directly related to the problem or to verses that will lead to a change in specific behavior having to do with the reason for which counseling is sought. The specific behavior sought by the counselor is often external and can be as mundane as taking out the trash or clearing the table after the meals. (See Part Two.)

In Christ-centered ministry the Bible verses used are primarily those that give the person a biblical perspective on trials, show how problems can be used for spiritual growth, and encourage a daily devotional life, whether or not the verses are directly related to the reason for which counseling is sought. The behavior sought by the one who ministers may be external, but is very often not directly related to the problem, but rather directed to building a daily devotional walk so that the person can grow spiritually and, as a result, deal with the problems. In most cases the one who grows spiritually is enabled to deal with the issues of life without needing counseling. (See Part Three.)

Most important to understand is that the central issue is the problem-centeredness of counseling systems that claim to be biblical, including those used by the National Association of Nouthetic Counselors (NANC) and the Christian Counseling and Educational Foundation (CCEF), which we critique later. The problem-centeredness that was cloned from the psychological counseling movement is central to what we are criticizing and recommending against. **Problem-centered counseling inevitably leads to sinful**

counseling. No matter how biblical one claims to be, so-called biblical counseling is defaulted by its problem-centeredness with its sinful communication and that includes NANC, CCEF, and other such organizations.

The Appeal of Problem-Centered Counseling

Problem-centered counseling appeals to the flesh of both the counselor and the counselee. The counselor gets to know the secrets of the counselee and learns about private matters that others are generally not privy to, which usually includes "juicy gossip" (talebearing) that appeals to the flesh. The counselor becomes the confidant of the counselee, very often hearing about private matters of the flesh, often at its worst, while not needing to reveal anything private about one's own life, marriage, family, thoughts, or behavior. Thus, the counselor gets to hear about the sins of others without having to reveal personal sin. The counselor appears as the expert who has it all together and who is able to fix the one who does not. It is a prideful and fleshly place to be. The appeal to the counselees' flesh exists because the counselees can present their case usually without being contradicted, condemned, or judged, but with gaining great sympathy and support.

The more directly problem-centered one becomes, the more self-centered the counseling is. **Problem-centeredness and self-centeredness are linked.** The client (i.e., the self) comes with a problem. The counseling is directed at the self with the problem. Thus, problem-centered counseling is actually self-centered counseling. The two are inextricably linked. In fact, just having the problem serves as an excuse for a person to receive a counselor's undivided attention. It would be appropriate to refer to this unbiblical activity as problem/self-centered counseling.

✗ Preaching, teaching, and evangelizing have been the basis for spiritual growth through the ages, not problem-centered counseling. However, just as the psychotherapists are looked up to as experts in the world, so too have their problem-centered biblical counseling counterparts been looked up to as experts in the church. The counselor is often regarded more highly than the pastor, and counseling is often regarded more highly than the teaching, preaching, and evangelizing. Instead of having a priesthood **of** all believers, counselors often become the priests **to** all believers. And, instead of the true priests from the priesthood of all believers exercising the cure of souls to one another, the biblical counselors have set themselves as priests in their soul-caring careers.

In her book *The Romance of American Psychology*, Ellen Herman reveals the power and prestige of psychological counselors, but notice how the same kudos apply to biblical counselors:

> Psychological insight is the creed of our time. In the name of enlightenment, experts promise help and faith, knowledge and comfort. They devise confident formulas for happy living and ambitious plans for dissolving the knots of conflict. Psychology, according to its boosters, possesses worthwhile answers to our most difficult personal questions and practical solutions for our most intractable social problems.[7]

Psychotherapists and biblical counselors, with their problem-centered preoccupation, are now regarded as the experts in the church as far as the issues of life, instead of the pastors, elders, evangelists, and fellow believers.

Problem-Centered Counseling Not Universal

Psychotherapy and problem-centered counseling are not universal throughout the world. It is a Western phenomenon.

Some non-Western countries are beginning to adopt it primarily because of Western influence. While it is on the increase, there has been little psychotherapy or counseling in East Asian countries. One major reason it is almost non-existent there is that East Asians are typically not self-oriented or personal-problem centered. They are typically **we-oriented**, while Westerners are typically **me-centered**. However, this is changing in these East Asian countries for two major reasons. (1) Asians go to American universities and learn about clinical psychology, change their major, get their degree in it, and go back to Asia to teach in higher education institutions or go into private practice counseling. (2) American missionaries take Western psychological concepts and practices to their mission fields.

The Rise of Problem-Centered Counseling

In our book *Christ-Centered Ministry versus Problem-Centered Counseling* we document the rise of problem-centered counseling in America. Through the influence of Franz Anton Mesmer devising his "magnetic" **talking cure**, Sigmund Freud searching for clues in the unconscious mind, and the Puritans searching for the idols of the heart, America became a cauldron of problem-centeredness as the royal road to mind cure.

Pastoral care has always been a part of the church. Historically pastoral care is referred to as "the cure of souls." In his book *A History of the Cure of Souls*, John T. McNeill says: "The cure of souls is, then, the sustaining and curative treatment of persons in those matters that reach beyond the requirements of animal life."[8] This "cure of souls" began early in the church with various writings on such aspects of the Christian life as grief, consolation, repentance, discipline, guidance, and growth. The medieval system emphasized legal restraint of external "sins" rather than sin residing in the inner man. The Protestant Reformation emphasized the inner man without ignoring the external expressions.

Dr. Thomas Szasz is one of the world's best-known and distinguished university professors of psychiatry. He is also one of the best-known critics of psychiatry and psychotherapy. Szasz says that "the true precursor of modern psychotherapy [is] the pastoral cure of souls"[9] Szasz concludes: "Actually, psychotherapy is a modern, scientific-sounding name for what used to be called the 'cure of souls.'"[10]

Modern origins of psychotherapy began with Franz Anton Mesmer, an 18th century Austrian physician who devised a means of bodily healing which was also used for mind healing. Mesmer began with bodily manipulation for healing, but later used conversation as a means of healing, because the mind was then considered to be the gateway to both bodily and mental healing. This seemingly minor change made a dramatic difference. This was the beginning of **conversation as the medium of mind cure and problem-centeredness as the method of mind cure**. Robert Fuller, in his book *Mesmerism and the American Cure of Souls*, says that Mesmerism was: "The first psychological system to provide individuals with curative services that have traditionally been classified under the rubric cure of souls."[11]

Szasz says:

> Insofar as psychotherapy as a modern "medical technique" can be said to have a discoverer, Mesmer was that person, Mesmer stands in the same sort of relation to Freud and Jung as Columbus stands in relation to Thomas Jefferson and John Adams. Columbus stumbled onto a continent that the founding fathers subsequently transformed into the political entity known as the United States of America. Mesmer stumbled onto

the literalized use of the leading scientific metaphor of his age for explaining and exorcising all manner of human problems and passions, a rhetorical device that the founders of modern depth psychology sub-sequently transformed into the pseudomedical entity known as psychotherapy.[12]

Szasz describes the dramatic and historic changes that occurred in the 18th and 19th centuries and then sums up by saying:

> With the decline of religion and the growth of science in the eighteenth century, the cure of (sinful) souls, which had been an integral part of the Christian religions, was recast as the cure of (sick) minds, and became an integral part of medical science.[13]

The words *sinful* and *sick* are his and mark the dramatic shift from the cure of souls to the cure of minds. It also was a dramatic shift from the sufficiency of Scripture (cure of souls) to the wisdom of man (cure of minds).

Sigmund Freud (1856-1939) furthered the idea of con-versation being the medium and problem-centeredness being the method of mind cure in the 19th and 20th centuries. Szasz says that Freud "defined listening and talking—that is, con-versation as therapy."[14] Szasz refers to the conversation of psychotherapy as "rhetoric." He says:

> In plain language, what do patient and psychothera-pist actually do? They speak and listen to each other. What do they speak about? Narrowly put, the patient speaks about himself, and the therapist speaks about the patient. In a broader sense, however, both also speak about other persons and about various matters of concern to their lives. The point is that each tries to move the other to see or do things in a certain way.

That is what qualifies their actions as fundamentally rhetorical. If the psychotherapist and his patient were not rhetoricians, they could not engage in the activity we now conventionally call *psychotherapy*.[15]

Thus problem-centered psychotherapy has Mesmeric and Freudian origins, and, though it has gone through up to almost 500 varieties, **it still exists essentially as rhetoric as remedy and conversation as therapy**.

This rhetoric as remedy and conversation as therapy became professionalized and placed in the hands of these new (at the time) practitioners. Those who followed eventually needed to become educated and licensed. It was a milestone in the history of psychology, and now this problem-centered talk therapy has been fully accepted in both the world and the church. These psychological sorcerers of the soul now set the standards for solutions of the soul—solutions that have not only been wholeheartedly embraced but also practiced and expected in the church.

The book titled *The Practice of Psychology: The Battle for Professionalism* begins with the fact that "The independent provision of psychological services was virtually nonexistent prior to and during World War II."[16] It reveals that "most psychology departments tended to look down on applied practitioners, feeling that the 'true psychologist' was the one functioning in an academic setting."[17] Herman describes the rise of psychological counseling in America. She says:

> Throughout the entire postwar era, the United States has trained and employed more psychological experts, per capita, than any other country in the world.... Before World War II, professional healers and counselors were few; most individuals allied with psychology did work unrelated to "helping."[18]

Herman describes the omnipresence of psychology as having "seeped into virtually every facet of existence," but she says, "that does not mean that it has always been there or that what experts say has always mattered as much as it matters today."[19]

Aside from individual meetings and brief advice giving, this problem-centered counseling mania did not exist in or out of the church prior to World War II. At the same time problem-centered counseling came in, the bar was lowered as to what constitutes problems that should lead to counseling. The bar was first lowered in the secular world through problem-centered counseling and then some years later the church followed suit. The bar that was lowered was what problems constitute a need for counseling for Christians.

With the rise of affluence after World War II, there was a shift from interest in the supernatural (spiritual) to the natural (fleshly) and from the eternal to the here and now. Instead of seeing the trials and tribulations of life as challenges to faith as a normal part of the Christian experience, and even as something to build endurance while looking ahead to a blessed eternity with God, there was an increased desire to seek present happiness through counseling. This also impacted the church where there was a shift from dependence upon God to a dependence upon self to deal with the trials of life. The wisdom of men became the standard of change, and counseling became the means to accomplish happiness here and now. In order to attain here and now happiness, people seek to have the normal twists and trials of life adjusted through problem-centered counseling. Thus the bar was not just lowered, but practically eliminated, when it came to what problems are fair game for the counselor's office.

In her chapter on "The Growth Industry," Herman describes how psychotherapy (problem-centered counseling) grew from treating those with extreme mood disorders to individuals who did not think of themselves as "mentally ill," but wanted what they regarded as the benefits of treatment. Herman concludes the chapter on growth with a section titled "Psychotherapy for the Normal as a Postwar Growth Industry." At the end of it she says:

> Each of the developments described in this chapter expanded psychology's jurisdiction applying the theories and technologies of clinical expertise to more people in more places for more reasons than before.... Strengthening feelings of human connection and identification, struggling to adjust, gain insight, and become fully human—these were gradually transformed into important social goals as well as widespread individual preoccupations during the postwar decades.[20]

Herman later says, **"As a result, psychological help was defined so broadly that everyone needed it"**[21] (bold added). In the last half of the 20th century the supposed need for psychological counseling and the practice of counseling psychology accelerated rapidly.

Problem-centered psychological counseling was first embraced by those Christians who became educated to be teachers or licensed practitioners and then embraced by those in the newly formed biblical counseling movement. **The activity of conversation as therapy and rhetoric as remedy is promulgated through problem-centered counseling, which is now the standard outside and inside the church; it is the standard in both psychological and biblical counseling.** A return to the true biblical way will be difficult to accomplish, but a drastic turnaround is necessary if spiritual growth is the goal rather than fleshly change.

Sketching the history of the rise of counseling psychology and its importance throughout America, Dr. Bernie Zilbergeld said, "It is probably not unfair to say that it [counseling psychology] has become as important as the tenets of Christianity once were."[22] Few will admit it, but in practice this is true throughout much of the church. And those in biblical counseling often mimic those in the psychological counseling movement with the same fixation on problem-centeredness and a whole panorama of problems never before considered worthy of such attention in the church.

Prior to World War II whoever thought of discussing problems as is currently done in problem-centered counseling and whoever knew that the most mundane aspects of life, never before regarded as worthy to be aired, would be the subjects of such conversations? For example, such "important" problem-centered marriage counseling topics as the husband "does not pick up his socks" and the wife "does not serve meals that please." (See Part Two.) **Eliminating talking about such trivial problems of living that have been magnified beyond significance by a self-centered, self-indulgent society seeking present-life, personal happiness would extinguish much of the plethora of problem-centered conversations.**

Oprah Winfrey, along with other media notables, accelerated psychological problem-centeredness and made it more public and more transparent than ever before. Winfrey and other media moguls earned the epithet of belonging to the "trash pack" to describe the trash talk content of their shows.[23] As one examines the sinful nature of biblical counseling conversations, a number of them sound like trash talk. To use a biblical term, trash talk is literally *sin*.

Christians now follow the sinful trash talk in its openness to speaking publicly about what formerly was either not spoken about at all or only mentioned in private to family members or church leaders. Whether it is admitted or not, biblical counseling problem-centered conversations are a clear reflection of the psychological sinful talk therapy mentality that has achieved such popularity through the media, higher education, politics, and elsewhere. The church has been deceived into passivity or is actively involved in this sinful trash talk by ignoring scriptures to the contrary (e.g., Eph. 4:29; Phil. 4:8; James 3:2-10). The biblical counseling movement needs to move out of their sinful problem-centeredness and on to a Christ-centeredness that will truly offer hope and an opportunity to transform lives rather than being stuck in sinful trash talk.

In the main, biblical counselors begin with a problem-centered mentality that was assimilated from the secular psychological counseling movement. Most of them never examine the limitations or even, in many instances, the biblical prohibitions against their practices; neither do many provide a biblical justification for what they do. As we demonstrate, problem-centered counseling as practiced by biblical counselors is absent from Scripture itself, as well as throughout the centuries that followed the New Testament church.[24]

Nowhere in Scripture can one find a counselor involved in the kinds of on-going, problem-centered conversations as those described in the numerous lectures and counseling manuals. In fact, as we have documented elsewhere and in this current book, there are biblical prohibitions against much of what transpires during those formatted and ongoing planned biblical counseling conversations.[25]

There are currently hundreds of biblical counseling books that advocate a counseling process, wherein **week after week**, the counselee describes the **problem**; the counselor asks questions about the **problem** for further clarification; suggestions are made about the **problem**; discussions center on the **problem**; Bible verses that may be related to the **problem** are given; and homework regarding the **problem** is assigned. The focus is continually on the **problem** and on talk, talk, talk and feelings, feelings, feelings. This pattern mimics the psychological counseling movement and is wholly without a biblical example and without a valid biblical justification. Problem-centered biblical counseling conversations often result in psychological speculations. The individuals who come repeatedly for problem-centered counseling are, in the main, shallow believers. We contend that there is an inverse correlation between the amount of problem-centered counseling in a church and the level of spirituality within the congregation. **In other words, if a church is loaded with problem-centered counseling, it is an indication of the low level of spirituality in a church and of poor teaching, preaching, and evangelizing there.**

Focusing on Negative Feelings

We know that considerable research dealing with what is called "Post-Traumatic Stress Disorder" (PTSD) indicates that those who receive treatment "do no better than those who don't and that a significant number of people treated ... do even worse than those who didn't receive treatment." Reporting on the extensive research, the writer says:

> This negative reaction seems to emerge because, for some people, **the very act of focusing on their negative feelings** ... increases their distress and leads to more difficulties, such as flashbacks, nightmares, and anxiety attacks (bold added).[26]

Using this as a hint, is it not possible that talking about problems, as in problem-centered counseling, is detrimental to those who seek relief by rehearsing, rehashing, reliving and regurgitating their problems? While problem-centered counseling does not always deal with PTSD, most counseling does involve "**the very act of focusing on ... negative feelings.**" This research conclusion about PTSD should by extension raise questions about problem-centered counseling.

Whether it is a couple or an individual, the scenario is quite similar. The problem, whatever it might be, is central to the conversation carried on and on. Because the counselor's role is problem solver, the problem-centered counselor has to know about the problem. The problem-centered counselor needs to hear the problem explained; try to understand it according to some theory or guesswork; and offer some kind of solution. En route to suggestions and assignments, if given, there will no doubt be a focus on negative feelings and thus there will be a violation of the biblical principles described in our past writings and in this current book.[27]

Self Justification

A recent secular book titled *Mistakes Were Made (But Not by Me): Why We Justify Foolish Beliefs, Bad Decisions, and Hurtful Acts* illustrates how evil and desperately wicked the heart is with respect to self justification for even the most evil acts and how people practice "**confirmational bias.**"[28] Confirmational bias occurs when people seek evidence that "confirms" their opinions or supports the decisions they make, while ignoring other contradictory information. Read the cases in counseling books and you will see how the truth of Jeremiah 17:9 plays out. **It is rare to find a person who will take responsibility for the problem without any "confirmational bias,"** i.e., resorting to the flesh, which is one more reason not to be involved in problem-centered counseling.

Marriage Counseling

Marriage counseling is big business in the world and in the church. As more and more people have been going to marriage counseling, more and more have become divorced, and this includes professing Christians, who are divorcing at about the same rate as unbelievers.[29] With all the time and money and the great expectations that counseling will help married couples, it is disconcerting to learn that marriage counseling only helps about half of the time, which is similar to sham treatment. Why are the results so poor? The editor of *Psychotherapy Networker,* a journal for practicing psychotherapists, confesses that "most therapists who actually do marital therapy (about 80 percent of all clinicians) don't really know what they're doing." He says:

> Untrained in and unprepared for work that requires a highly skilled touch and nerves of steel, many therapists blunder ineffectually through sessions until they're fired by their clients or, overwhelmed by a couple's problems, they give up too soon in trying to save a marriage.[30]

But then he admits that skilled, experienced therapists are often unsuccessful as well. We believe that the lack of success is because of problem-centered counseling that requires problems to be known by outsiders and where each spouse airs complaints about the other or about the relatives or other third parties session after session. This lack of success in psychological counseling is no doubt repeated in biblical counseling because both approaches focus on repeatedly revealing and dealing with problems in the presence or absence of a spouse under the leadership of a counselor. (See Part Two.)

The area of marriage counseling is a prime example of how unbiblical and problem-centered biblical counseling can be. Christian couples who enter biblical counseling are typically allowed to discuss problems over and over again in the same manner as they would with mental health professionals. Their problems, especially with one another, become the center of the interchange. **Most counselors would not know what to do without problems being discussed.** However, Ephesians 5 should restrict any couple from continually exposing one another's faults and failures in front of a biblical counselor or anyone else, **unless there are extreme circumstances that need to be confronted immediately**. No counselor who ministers biblically should permit such a problem-centered activity to occur again and again or enable such sinful communication. Instead, when such problem-centered biblical violations occur, they should serve as reminders to divert away from self and problems and towards teaching biblical doctrines and understandings. Ongoing complaints about one another typically exacerbate problem-ridden marriages and violate Ephesians 5. Those who are Christ-centered helpers will avoid such dialogue. (See Part Three.)

3. Working on the Outside: Behaviorism

Problem-centered biblical counselors who attempt to change behavior often follow a **works-oriented, unbiblical psychological behaviorism** where the focus is on overt behavior and the removal or change in overt symptoms. In other words, they attempt to transform a person from the outside-in. They work on behavior with the idea that change in external behavior will bring forth internal right feelings, attitudes, and spiritual change. They say, "If you **do** right, you will **feel** right."

Scripture does not present outward conformity to what is right as being sufficient or as being a way to change the inner man. Jesus chastised the Pharisees for being "whited sepulchers." The Pharisees appeared to do right in their external behavior, but were not right internally. Jesus said:

> Woe unto you, scribes and Pharisees, hypocrites! for ye are like unto whited sepulchres, which indeed appear beautiful outward, but are within full of dead men's bones, and of all uncleanness. Even so ye also outwardly appear righteous unto men, but within ye are full of hypocrisy and iniquity (Matt. 23:27,28).

If any group could be used to demonstrate whether or not outward change produces inner change, it would be the Pharisees.

In both salvation and sanctification God is working on the inside and there is an inner response of faith, which precedes external change. As the apostle Paul explains:

> For by grace are ye saved through faith; and that not of yourselves: it is the gift of God: not of works, lest any man should boast. For we are his workmanship, created in Christ Jesus unto good works, which God hath before ordained that we should walk in them (Eph. 2:8-10).

Yes, there is to be outer change, but that change is wrought first on the inside by grace through faith.

Nouthetic counseling, mentioned earlier, is one of the more popular counseling approaches. The organization that promotes this primarily behavioral approach is the National Association of Nouthetic Counselors (NANC). A clear example of the behavioristic nature of nouthetic counseling comes from a plenary talk at a national meeting of NANC. The featured speaker was one of their board members.[31] Regarding pride, this NANC board member asked his audience that, if anyone **saw** pride in him, to bring it to his attention. He went on to say, "If it even looks like it [pride], bring it to my attention." In other words, pride could apparently be diagnosed overtly in what the audience "saw" in the speaker. His emphasis on the outward behavior, "If it even **looks** like," also reveals the behavioristic approach of this brand of biblical counseling. We think it fair to say that pride is primarily a matter of the human heart. This speaker, who is now a seminary professor, trains others in this behavioristic system.

There are numerous examples of this type of approach in the biblical counseling movement. While Scripture is used, it is used as a means to change external behavior. There are numerous books about being a better wife, being a better husband, having a better marriage, overcoming addictions, anxiety, etc. While many sound biblical doctrines may be taught in these books, their counseling is problem-centered. The methods and techniques are aimed at changing external behavior or eliminating symptoms. These represent a behavioristic approach to changing behavior. We critique this approach in Part Two.

4. Working on the Inside: Inner Workings of the Heart

Another way problem-centered biblical counselors attempt to bring about change reflects various forms of insight therapy, in which the counselor attempts to know what is on the inside that is driving present feelings and behavior. These biblical counselors seek to identify the inner workings of the heart. Indeed, they are looking for change in the right place, on the inside. However, when humans attempt to look inside another person they enter a guessing game. Some connect certain outward expressions of behavior with what they call **"idols of the heart"** and then attempt to help individuals confront their particular idols of the heart. However, most is like insight therapy—searching the inner man through conversation and guessing about what is there. Instead of moving the person closer to the Lord for Him to work on the inside, they try to help the person by giving their own ideas (guesses based on their own perceptions) as to what is going on inside. Only the Lord can see inside a person. His Word declares. "The heart is deceitful above all things, and desperately wicked: who can know it? I the LORD search the heart, I try the reins, even to give every man according to his ways, and according to the fruit of his doings" (Jer. 17:9-10).

Inner-workings-of-the-heart counseling is not like a Catholic confessional where one confesses a known sin; it is an exploration of a person's inner caverns to discover the hidden intentions of the heart. In using this approach, many in the biblical counseling movement treat the inner workings of the heart somewhat like the Freudian unconscious, and it can very easily become similar to what a psychoanalyst does in probing the unconscious. There are those in the BCM who probe the "unconscious" of the heart, but there is **no biblical justification for this understanding of the heart in Scripture.**

This inner-workings-of-the-heart approach is best exemplified at the Christian Counseling and Educational Foundation (CCEF). While there may be slight variations of how each member of the CCEF counselors counsel, they are primarily inner-workings-of-the-heart directed. Examples of this are seen in *The Journal of Biblical Counseling*, in their books, and in their talks and conferences. A lengthy article by Dr. David Powlison in *The Journal of Biblical Counseling*, a CCEF publication, explains his understanding of the inner workings of the heart through what he calls "**the idols of the heart**," the diagnosis of which is the basis of his problem-centered approach.[32] (See Part Two.)

Instead of focusing on problems or attempting to expose the heart, a pastor and congregation should be involved in active sanctification, growing in the fruit of the Spirit, learning to walk according to the Spirit, with Jesus being the center of attention, and becoming more like Him the goal. The Bible reveals spiritual issues that underlie behavior. Thus it is entirely unnecessary and unscriptural to use psychological techniques or some biblical sounding, idols-of-the-heart methods to gain insight into the inner man or to expose the heart, which is the domain of the Holy Spirit, not of man!

Caring for Souls Inside and Out

The care of souls does involve the inner person. But such work is **not** done by "counselors" analyzing another person's inner life. What we can do for each other continues to be what is given throughout the New Testament. We can teach, preach, testify, exhort, encourage, come alongside, speak the truth in love, rebuke, identify external sin, correct, comfort, forgive, and pray. These are the activities that Scripture says minister to both the inner and outer person.

Humans may guess at the inner workings of another person's heart by observing external sin, but, even with external evidence, they may be drawing the wrong conclusions. If there is sin, one may identify it as an idol of the heart, which is an ambiguous term that can have a variety of meanings. However, it is more clearly biblical to express it as the love of the world manifesting itself in "the lust of the flesh, and the lust of the eyes, and the pride of life" (1 John 2:16). Moreover, the way out is not through one person, called "counselor," peering inside the heart of another person, called "counselee," to identify and analyze. True change is brought about by God working in the individual. As He is doing something miraculous in a believer's heart, He uses the external efforts of believers teaching, preaching, testifying, exhorting, encouraging, coming alongside, speaking the truth in love, identifying external sin, rebuking, correcting, comforting, forgiving, praying, helping in practical matters of life, and being living examples of walking in the Spirit. We are not left with superficial, external help. Instead, God calls us to minister to one another on the human level while He accomplishes the miraculous inner work of the soul.

Biblical counselors are generally behaviorists, inner-workings-of-the-heart analysts, or a combination of the two. Both directions are problem-centered and miss the true biblical care of souls. While those who are working on the outside are not entirely behaviorists, that is their main focus. While those who are working on the inside are not entirely inner-focused, that is their main orientation. All are problem-centered!

5. Counselor, Counselee, Counseling

In speaking about the practices of the biblical counseling movement, we use the terms *counselor*, *counselee*, and *counseling* because it is their terminology. The three words *counselor, counselee,* and *counseling* are the three most popular terms to describe who does the counseling, who receives the counseling, and the activity of conversation known as counseling. **As used in the biblical counseling movement, not one of these individuals (counselor, counselee) and activities (counseling) is found in Scripture.**

Neither the Old nor the New Testament has an equivalent for the word *counselee*. In fact, the word *counselee* did not show up in a dictionary until 1934, when it was defined in the *Oxford English Dictionary* as "One who receives professional counselling." No wonder it is nowhere in the Bible. Psychological counseling created the need for a word to designate those receiving "professional counseling." Yet biblical counselors consistently call their recipients "counselees." Furthermore, those in the biblical counseling movement refuse to remove this one word from their vocabulary.

We discuss the biblical meanings and use of the equivalents to the words *counselor* and *counseling* and conclude that **there is no counseling found in the Bible as it is presently conducted by those who call themselves biblical counselors.**[33] It is misleading to use biblical words and give them a new meaning to defend the practice of contemporary biblical counseling. Just because the word is the same does not mean that they are doing the same thing. Same words do not equal the same practice. If the activities are called "biblical counseling," then the words and activities should be biblical. To use words from Scripture in a way that those words are not used in Scripture is confusing at least and deceptive at worst. This is compounded by biblically rationalizing the activity of contemporary problem-centered biblical counseling where no such biblical examples exist. For instance, in checking all the instances of counseling in the Bible, there is no example of a woman or couple being counseled or of a man being counseled regarding the kinds of personal problems discussed in biblical counseling. Thus, the terms used are from secular counseling and should be avoided by all who desire to be truly biblical in ministering to others. **The evidence from the Old and New Testaments is provided in Appendices A and B.**

Dr. Jay Adams' Use of the Words
Counsel and *Counseling*

One of the rationalizations given by Adams for using the term *counsel* is as follows:

> Because the New Testament term [*noutheteo*] is larger than the English word "counsel," and because it doesn't carry any of the "freight" that is attached to the latter term, we have simply imported the biblical term into English.[34]

In his article "What is Biblical Counseling?" Adams uses the following four verses from the Bible to describe his methodology and practice of counseling. He translates *noutheteo* uniquely here and in his own translation of the New Testament, titled *The Christian Counselor's New Testament,*[35] with the words *counsel* and *counseling*, to apply these words to his system of counseling:

> Romans 15:14: "I myself am convinced about you, my brothers, that you yourselves are full of goodness, filled with all knowledge, and competent to **counsel** one another."

> 1 Thessalonians 5:12: "Now we ask you, brothers, to recognize those who labor among you, and manage you in the Lord, and **counsel** you."

> 1 Corinthians 4:14: "I am not writing these things to shame you, but to **counsel** you as my dear children."

> Acts 20:31: "Therefore, be alert, remembering that for three years, night and day, I didn't stop **counseling** each one of you with tears."

Adams says that the Greek verb *noutheteo* and noun *nouthesia* are "sometimes translated 'admonish, correct or instruct.'" Nevertheless, he **uniquely** chooses to translate these words as *counsel* and *counseling*. While some versions translate the Greek verb as *warn*, **we found no other version that translated *noutheteo* and *nouthesia* as *counsel* and *counseling*.** We checked these four verses with numerous versions of the English Bible, excluding amplified and paraphrased versions, and **found no support for Adams' translation of these Greek words as *counsel* and *counseling*.** We also used an expository dictionary and a Greek-English lexicon and again **found no support for Adams' translation using the words *counsel* and *counseling*.**[36]

As we have said before, the word *counsel* as used by both psychological and biblical counselors carries a great deal of baggage. Moreover, no word translated as *counsel* in the Bible ever meant anything close to what goes on in present-day counseling where two or three people meet to talk about one person's or one couple's problems, complaints, feelings, and behavior week after week, where the focus of the conversation is the *counselee* (newly created word for the recipient of professional counseling during the 20th century) and the counselee's problems.

Adams also translates the following passages with *counsel* or a derivative:

> *noutheteo* as *counseling* in Acts 20:31; Col. 1:28;
>
> *noutheteo* as *counsel* Romans 15:14; 1 Cor. 4:14; Col. 3:16; 1 Thes. 5: 12,14; 2 Thes. 3:15;
>
> *nouthesia* as *counseling* in Titus 3:10.

Adams says, "The three ideas found in the word *nouthesia* are **Confrontation**, **Concern**, and **Change**"[37] (emphasis his). However, **none of those words are found as translations of the word *nouthesia* in the numerous versions of**

the Bible we checked. While Adams' form of counseling may include admonishment, correction, and instruction at times, there is also a great deal more that goes on, including many unbiblical practices we discuss in this Part One and in Part Two.

The words *counsel* and *counseling* in the BCM, as we have just indicated, resemble secular counseling, **not** what Jesus and Paul did. We think it more accurate to say that the words *noutheteo* and *nouthesia* were hijacked from the New Testament and transformed into *counsel* and *counseling* to give a biblical justification for what those who call themselves "biblical counselors" do and to avoid the obvious relationship to secular counseling with the "freight" that accompanies it.

New Testament Gifts and Callings

Where is the office of counselor in the New Testament? Is there a specific calling of counselor as there is for evangelists, pastors and teachers? Are there specific offices for a counselor as there are for elders and deacons? Why is the position of counselor absent, for instance, in Ephesians 4, which speaks of Christ's gifts to the church:

> And he gave some, apostles; and some, prophets; and some, evangelists; and some, pastors and teachers; For the perfecting of the saints, for the work of the ministry, for the edifying of the body of Christ: Till we all come in the unity of the faith, and of the knowledge of the Son of God, unto a perfect man, unto the measure of the stature of the fulness of Christ (Eph. 4:11-13).

Romans 12:4-13 describes the function of the Body of Christ with members using their spiritual gifts for the spiritual benefit of one another:

> For as we have many members in one body, and all
> members have not the same office: So we, being
> many, are one body in Christ, and every one members
> one of another. Having then gifts differing according
> to the grace that is given to us (vv. 4-6a).

Note all that is accomplished through these gifts of
ministry described throughout these passages. With the great
emphasis on counseling today, it is amazing that "counselor"
is not in the list. Through all the gifts of ministry, along with
the Word of God and the Holy Spirit, the saints would be
perfected, that is, become mature in the faith. They would
be equipped to do the "work of the ministry," they would be
built up, they would come to unity based on their common
faith in the Lord Jesus Christ, and they would increase in
their knowledge of Christ. Moreover, through those gifts
of ministry, they would be so established in truth that they
would not be deceived (Eph. 4:14).

Besides the gifts of ministry, there is the Body of Christ
"fitly joined together and compacted by that which every joint
supplieth, according to the effectual working in the measure
of every part, maketh increase of the body unto the edifying
of itself in love" (Eph. 4:16). Here is where the one-to-one
ministry occurs: the one-another edifying, encouraging, and
supplying what is needed—the mutual caring, giving, and
loving—occurring as naturally as the different parts of the
human body work together for health and well-being. There
is no one-up/one-down relationship of counselor and "counselee." Instead there is the mutual care, encouragement, and
edification of all members of the Body of Christ. Counsel
may be given and received, but **the real position of counselor is reserved for the Holy Spirit**, who indwells every
believer, who sees into the inner man, who applies the Word
and makes it effectual in the believer, and then who enables

the believer to glorify God through love and obedience, as most clearly taught in Romans 8:26-27:

> Likewise the Spirit also helpeth our infirmities: for we know not what we should pray for as we ought: but the Spirit itself maketh intercession for us with groanings which cannot be uttered. And he that searcheth the hearts knoweth what is the mind of the Spirit, because he maketh intercession for the saints according to the will of God.

It has been said by some, and we agree, that those who take the position of counselor in someone else's life may be usurping the role of the Holy Spirit. Believers are called to comfort (1 Thessalonians 5:11), instruct (2 Timothy 2:24-26), edify (Romans 14:19), admonish (Romans 15:14), forgive (Ephesians 4:32), and restore (Galatians 6:1) one another. However, the only one who can accurately see inside a person and therefore be the real counselor is the Lord Himself.

Rather than emphasizing counseling, the Scriptures emphasize teaching. For instance, Paul wrote to Timothy: "And the things that thou hast heard of me among many witnesses, the same commit thou to faithful men, who shall be able to teach others also" (2 Timothy 2:2). The older women were to teach the younger women: "To be discreet, chaste, keepers at home, good, obedient to their own husbands, that the word of God be not blasphemed" (Titus 2:5).

Some biblical counselors claim that they are simply teachers or that they are simply discipling other believers. If that is the case, why do they call themselves "counselors" and why do they follow the format of worldly counseling? While we see instances of teaching in Scripture, such instances do not resemble the process of counseling as it is practiced today, with weekly problem-centered appointments.

The word translated *teachers* is *didaskalos*. If teaching is what they do, why not call it "biblical teaching" instead of "biblical counseling"? By picking up the word *counselor*, the rest of the baggage comes along. And, counseling is a big attraction. As we said earlier, that's where the prestige is in Christendom today. Counselors are often held in higher regard than pastors, both inside and outside the church. The desire is for an expert in understanding human problems and how to deal with them. **The assumption is that the trained counselor has special knowledge. The unspoken implication is that the pastor does not.**

The special knowledge people seem to be looking for has to do with the soul itself, rather than external behavior. As we said earlier, among the biblical counselors there are those who counsel behavioristically and those who counsel analytically as they attempt to identify the idols of the heart. There are those who look for the answers to people's problems in their past and in their "unconscious." There are those who believe Christians can be demon possessed and claim expertise at exorcism. And, there are those who counsel according to the four temperaments and their varied offshoots. The notions and nuances of biblical counseling range from incorporating aspects of secular counseling to engaging in unbiblical supernatural experimentation. Just as there are numerous different forms of psychological therapy with individual therapists practicing their own combination, so too with biblical counseling. While some have attempted to control the field through certificates, diplomas, degrees, and organizations, there is no single model or method of biblical counseling. **Each counselor uses the Bible according to some combination of personal experience, secular theories, biblical doctrines, and "common sense." The common thread among them all is their problem-centeredness.**

While those who call themselves "biblical counselors" may be operating according to Scripture to some degree, they do so **not** within a position delineated in Scripture, because the New Testament does not present the position of the contemporary counselor. If they do minister biblically to another believer, they do so simply as fellow believers or within ordained ministries presented in Scripture. The replacement for psychological counseling is not biblical counseling. It is ministering the Word of God to one another in love, patience, and forbearance. It involves believers being equipped through the gifts of ministry. Moreover, the Lord Himself eliminates the need for a psychological or biblical counselor.

Our society places great value on the position of counselor. If the common name for a psychotherapist were "advisor" and the activity were called "advising," those would probably be the very words adopted by the church. Instead of "biblical counselors," there would be "biblical advisors" doing "biblical advising." If those terms sound dull and flat, it's because the powerful symbol is *counselor*, not *advisor*. An example of the centrality of biblical counseling over and above normal pastoral practice can be seen in the name change from *The Journal of Pastoral Practice* to *The Journal of Biblical Counseling*.

Counselor, *counselee*, and *counseling* are words that have been empowered and given status by a secular therapeutic society and adopted by the biblical counseling movement. These three terms are imbedded in the fabric of the secular society and provide a façade of culturally sanctioned assets to the biblical counseling movement. They give an air of "professionalism" to the practice of biblical counseling. As secular and unbiblical as they are, the biblical counselors refuse to give them up and replace them with biblical terms and practices.

Christians need to move away from using the designations "biblical counseling" and "biblical counselor." The words *counseling* and *counselor* have become powerful symbols and suffer the same shortcomings within the church as they do outside the church. Because the terms *counsel* (verb form), *counselor*, *counselee*, and *counseling* have such strong roots, meanings, and ties to psychotherapy with no biblical basis for their use in ministry, we suggest replacing them with the following:

counsel	minister, evangelize, teach, pastor, disciple, come alongside, advise, encourage, admonish, exhort
counselor	minister, evangelist, teacher, pastor, fellow believer, helper, elder, brother, sister, the one who ministers
counselee	fellow believer, brother, sister (or, if not a believer, a possible convert), person, individual
counseling	ministering, pastoring, evangelizing, teaching, encouraging, exhorting, admonishing, advising

While some of these terms are not in Scripture, at least they are not contaminated by association with the psychological counseling movement and are in harmony with what Scripture teaches.

6. The Biblical Ideal

The following presents what would be the biblical ideal. Ideally there would be no talebearing, inappropriate (often sinful) discussion (such as in marriage counseling), blaming the past, playing the victim, or dishonoring parents, as described in the following sections. Thankfully there is the exceptional person who accepts responsibility for the problem and seeks advice as to what to do in accordance with God's Word. However, practically speaking, almost every person and couple to whom we have ministered wants to describe the problem and have it fixed quickly. Typically and rightly or wrongly, the person sees someone else or external circumstances as being the reason for the problem. We do listen to all who desire our help but will divert as quickly as possible from their problem-centeredness, especially if they violate biblical admonitions.

Our goal is to move them from problem-centeredness to Christ-centeredness as rapidly as possible. We may give advice regarding what the person may do or change according to Scripture, but then we will move the conversation away from the problem and onto Christ. **While there are many other violations of Scripture that often occur during problem-centered counseling, we discuss only talebearing, inappropriate (often sinful) discussion (such as in marriage counseling), blaming the past, playing the victim, and dishonoring parents.** These are five of many sins in which problem-centered counselors are often involved and which are discussed in the following and dealt with again in Part Two and Part Three, which also provides suggestions for how to divert from problem-centeredness to Christ-centeredness.

7. Talebearing

What do people talk about in counseling? They talk about themselves, their feelings, their relationships, their problems, and other people in their lives. In problem-centered counseling people often talk about their parents, spouse, children, other relatives, and close friends, as well as numerous other people. What might they be saying? More often than not, the counselee will talk about people who are not present. While there may be no intentional lying, the story will be told from the teller's perspective, with details chosen from the teller's memory. And because of the nature of memory, the story is rarely an exact replica of the events. Therefore it often turns into a tale that places the teller in a better light than the others being talked about.

Problem-centered counseling encourages talebearing. Think about any counseling you may have experienced or any groups that may have encouraged transparency. Quite often the very act of individual or group counseling will involve participants saying personal things about other people who are not present. That often involves talebearing—spreading gossip, secrets, biased impressions, and so forth about others who are not present. In fact, counseling often encourages such talebearing as the counselor elicits details and continually searches for clues as to the whys and wherefores of what is troubling the individual. After all, many problems of living involve other people.

When we warn about gossip and dishonoring, we do not condone covering up actual serious sins that may have been committed, but those would have to be verified, not just talked about in counseling. If an actual crime has been committed, the person may need to report the crime to the authorities, not just talk about it in counseling.

What the Bible Says

The Bible warns us about the evil of talebearing: "The words of a talebearer are as wounds, and they go down into the innermost parts of the belly" (Proverbs 18:8; 26:22); "He that goeth about *as* a talebearer revealeth secrets: therefore meddle not with him that flattereth with his lips" (Proverbs 20:19); "Where no wood is, *there* the fire goeth out: so where *there is* no talebearer, the strife ceaseth" (Proverbs 26:20). Moreover, the Lord commands His people not to act as talebearers: "Thou shalt not go up and down *as* a talebearer among thy people" (Lev. 19:16).

Complaining about other people during counseling will generally give a very biased view. As the counselor hears the ongoing complaints, he cannot help but form an impression of the person being complained about. The counselor is hearing only one side of the story and would tend to see the situation from that perspective.

When talebearing includes false information about another person, it becomes bearing false witness. "Thou shalt not bear false witness against thy neighbour" (Exodus 20:16; see also Deut. 5:20; Ps. 101:5; Prov. 24:28). Bearing false witness in counseling can happen as a person describes situations from a hurt and biased perspective. Sometimes a person is covering his own sin by exaggerating the sins of others and finding fault in areas that would not even be considered sinful, such as annoying habits. Tainted tales about other people are grievous. Proverbs 25:18 says, "A man that beareth false witness against his neighbour *is* a maul, and a sword, and a sharp arrow."

How many counselors actually check out the details of the stories they have been told? Very few, if any. In fact, recovered memory counselors contend that it is their duty to believe and support the counselee, even though research has demonstrated not only that memory is faulty, but also that counselees lie to their counselors. Many counselees deceive by telling only part of the story and thereby turn it into talebearing. The Bible advises getting the facts before believing tales: "He that is first in his own cause seemeth just; but his neighbour cometh and searcheth him" (Prov. 18:17).

The problem-centered counseling mentality has spread far beyond the counselors' offices. The mentality that considers talking about problems and about other people as being necessary is pandemic in our culture. Gossip is as old as the Fall and talebearing gets lots of attention for the flesh. Indeed, people love to gossip and to tell tales. Not only do they get lots of attention, but when they tell their tales from their own perspective, they may get lots of sympathy and support. Yes, indeed, the flesh may feel better. In fact, people often feel relieved to "get it off their chest," but the feeling of relief does not make it right or even helpful to the situation. The very process of counseling encourages people to talk about other people unnecessarily. Those who claim to be biblical counselors who encourage people to talk about others cannot be performing a biblically-sound service.

Is This Kind of Talk Necessary?

This kind of talk not only happens in problem-centered counseling; it is encouraged! Even Christians who write so-called case studies that may be composites of more than one case include details about relationships that they should have no business knowing, but which are expected and encouraged in counseling. For years people have been told that it is good to talk about their problems and to share personal details about others. Somehow talking about these things has been promoted as necessary for mental-emotional healing, even though no research supports that claim. Actually, some people feel worse because the problems may appear bigger after discussing and analyzing them. Once a person describes a spouse in negative terms it is difficult to see the positive qualities, because positive qualities might undermine what has been said to the therapist. Rather than the attitude about the situation improving, there is a strong possibility that the attitude may become strongly attached to the description given to the counselor. A felt need to justify one's complaints may solidify the negative report given to the counselor and lead to further deterioration in the relationship.

Is it possible to help people without the sins of others who are not present being exposed? Is it possible to help people without talebearing? Is it possible to help people without focusing on problems? (See Part Three.) After all, some people, especially women, may temporarily feel better after they have talked with a sympathetic listener (counselor) about problem people in their lives. But, this feeling of unburdening oneself is short-lived and, in itself, does not solve the problems. In fact, problems often get worse, because, when people repeatedly spend emotional energy thinking and talking about what bothers them about their circumstances and other people, the problems draw so much attention that what is good and right fades into the background. Even if a person does feel better knowing that someone else has heard and cared, can ongoing counseling that encourages or even allows talebearing be the right way to help someone when talebearing can be harmful and is forbidden in Scripture?

Problem-centered counseling often encourages talebearing; biblical ministry does not. **If talebearing and gossip were eliminated from ongoing, week-after-week counseling, many counselors would not know what to talk about, what to do, or how to handle the problem situation.**

8. Discussing Marital Problems

With certain exceptions, it is sinful to discuss marital problems with others or to complain about one's spouse to someone in each other's presence or absence (Eph. 5:21, 22,

25; Prov. 18:17). She talks about him when he's not there; he talks about her when she's not there; or they talk about one another in front of the counselor. In problem-centered counseling biblical counselors not only listen to ongoing complaints, but often encourage such expression.

Personal or marital problem-centered counseling encourages one to expose sins, secrets, or private matters of others not present and is often dependent on talebearing. If a woman complains about her husband in counseling or elsewhere, she is very possibly revealing private matters, exposing perceived or actual faults, and/or making him seem worse than he really is. If a husband complains about his wife in counseling, or elsewhere, he is very possibly revealing private matters, exposing perceived or actual faults, and/or making her seem worse than she really is. Talebearing harms relationships and may be one of the main reasons marriage counseling so often leads to divorce. Those who love one another will rarely share private matters about another person with others, including biblical counselors.

Violating the One Flesh of Marriage

Marriage provides many opportunities for spiritual growth. But instead of using these constructively, partners in problem-centered counseling often focus on problems, blame each other, and want the other partner or circumstances to change. Instead of seeking the Lord to work in their own lives, they go to problem-centered counseling, talk about their problems, and expect the counselor to do something (change circumstances or the other partner). Quite often people want the counselor to help the other partner see their point of view. If the counseling does not fix the problems, the people feel they have done everything they can, figure there is no hope for change, and move into the direction of separation and/or divorce—all at the expense of their precious children's well-being. What does the Bible say?

> Submitting yourselves one to another in the fear of the Lord (Eph. 5:21).

> Wives, submit yourselves unto your own husbands, as unto the Lord (Eph. 5:22).

> Husbands, love your wives, even as Christ also loved the church, and gave himself for it (Eph. 5:25).

Based on these verses, we conclude that the following problem-centered counseling activities violate the biblical one-flesh principle:

1. **Discussing marital problems with others or complaining about one's spouse in each other's presence.** If a husband is loving his wife as Christ loves the church, he will not be exposing her weaknesses and failures to others (including the children). If the wife is honoring her husband, submitting to him (as the church to Christ) and loving him (Titus 2:3-4), she will not be exposing his weaknesses and failures to others (including the children). Of course, there are necessary exceptions, such as physical or sexual abuse in a family or such sin as pornography, illegal drug use, or drunkenness, which should be brought to the attention of the church leadership and cases where civil laws have been broken may need to be brought to the attention of civil authorities.

2. **Discussing marital problems with others or complaining about one's spouse in his/her absence.** Proverbs 18:17 says, "He that is first in his own cause seemeth just; but his neighbour cometh and searcheth him" (Prov. 18:17). Very often one

spouse will attempt to get a counselor or friend to see a situation from that perspective by talking about the other spouse in his/her absence. The one who is first to state the case may gain support from the counselor or friend, but the truth may be revealed later. Furthermore, this can lead to a further rift in the marriage relationship. It ends up being the kind of gossip that separates people. Proverbs 17:9 advises, "He that covereth a transgression seeketh love; but he that repeateth a matter separateth very friends."

3. **Discussing marital problems with others for the purpose of getting a spouse to change.** If people are in a personal conflict with another person and believe that it is primarily the other person's fault, they are wasting a valuable opportunity if they are trying to change the other person or simply hoping for the other person to change. Such conflict can be an exceptional opportunity for spiritual growth. If one's eyes are on the other person and that person's need for change, one can get bogged down and waste the opportunity.

Every problem in life is an opportunity for spiritual growth (Romans 5:1-5; Romans 8:28-29). So often believers pray for God to change the other person when they themselves are in a perfect place to draw close to the Lord, to come to know Him more deeply, and to love Him more completely. All believers have numerous opportunities to focus on their own relationship with Christ, to look to Him to work in their own lives for spiritual growth, and to confess their own sins rather than the shortcomings and failures of others. Shifting the focus to how others must change defeats the purpose of spiritual transformation and growth (see Genesis 3:12-13).

9. Blaming the Past

Blaming the past is one of the major themes of Freudian and other insight-oriented psychotherapies. By permitting and participating in such problem-centered counseling, the biblical counselor is clearly being unbiblical (Phil. 3:13, 14). For years the counseling way of dealing with problems of living has been to talk about the problems, feelings, circumstances, and the sins of others, including family members. Because many counseling theories consider one's childhood to be the source of later problems, much time may be devoted to looking for ways that parents and other adults failed to give the child exactly what the counselee or counselor thinks the child needed at the time.

Some problem-centered counselors encourage the counselee to remember and even re-experience the past. Since recall is never truly accurate, but rather is full of gaps that must be filled in, the memory inevitably becomes altered and enhanced. The further back the memory, the greater chance for imagination to take over and the greater the inaccuracy. As these tales unfold and are emotionally experienced, they take on a life of their own and become newly created memories—tales of parents doing things they never did or failing to do what they actually did.

There is no biblical basis for such use of the past (as determinants of present behavior). The Bible includes the past works of God in history, because we are to remember the works of God both individually and corporately. But, regarding the Christian walk, the cross took care of the past. The walk of the believer is to be according to the new life and is therefore present and future oriented. In Philippians 3 Paul gives his religious and personal background, on which he had depended for righteousness before God. But when confronted by Jesus he saw his own wretched sinfulness, not only that he had persecuted the church, but that he was sinful to the core. He knew he could not make himself righteous by going back into his past. Therefore he declared: "This one thing I do, forgetting those things which are behind, and reaching forth unto those things which are before, I press toward the mark for the prize of the high calling of God in Christ Jesus" (Phil. 3:13-14). This does not mean an inability to recall the past; it means that the past now has a different significance. **Biblically speaking, attempting to fix the past is purely a fleshly activity that wars against the Spirit.**

A person need not be trapped in negative patterns of behavior established in the early years of life, for the Bible offers a new way of life. Put off the old man; put on the new. Jesus said to Nicodemus, "Ye must be born again" (John 3:7), and He said elsewhere that new wine could not be put into old wineskins (Matt. 9:17). Jesus offers new life and new beginnings. One who is born again has the spiritual capacity to overcome old ways and develop new ones through the action of the Holy Spirit, the fruit of the Spirit, and the sanctification of the believer. One wonders why so many have given up the hope of Christianity for the hopelessness of past determinism.

Turning to the past to find reasons for present problems, as often happens in problem-centered counseling, places blame on others and on circumstances rather than on one's own responsibilities and possibilities. Because of the nature of memory, remembering the past cannot be done without enhancing, embellishing, omitting, or creating details to fill in the blanks. Therefore, this is a faulty method of help because of the brain's limited ability to remember accurately and its tendency to distort.

Christ dealt with every believer's past at the cross when he died for their sins. When believers identify with Christ's death and resurrection they are free from the past of the flesh as well as the power of the flesh. They have a new life in Christ and are to live according to that new life. **Attempts to heal the hurts of the past are futile because one is not to heal that which is to be counted dead and buried.** Such sinful attempts give power to the flesh and will result in fleshly living in place of walking according to the Spirit. **Christ-centered ministry will encourage and help a seeker to leave the past at the foot of the cross and to "press toward the mark for the prize of the high calling of God in Christ Jesus"** (Phil. 3:14).

10. Playing the Victim

Problem-centered counseling sets the stage for playing the victim and blaming others, instead of recognizing the deceitfulness of one's own heart. There are individuals who are truly victims, but concentrating on their victimhood has never been a beneficial means of recovering from it.

Today there is a whole culture of victimhood way beyond those who have suffered serious tragedies. One book describes America as *A Nation of Victims*. The subtitle is *The Decay of the American Character*. According to the book's description, "The plaint of the victim—*It's not my fault*—has become the loudest and most influential voice in America." The author, Charles Sykes says:

> The ethos of victimization has an endless capacity not only for exculpating one's self from blame, washing away responsibility in a torrent of explanation—racism, sexism, rotten parents, addiction, and illness—but also for projecting guilt onto others.[38]

Sykes also says, "The impulse to flee from personal responsibility and blame others seems far more deeply embedded within the American culture."[39] He explains, "Increasingly, Americans act as if they had received a lifelong indemnification from misfortune and a contractual release from personal responsibility."[40]

The many biblical counselors who are problem-centered often both hear and support the prevalent victim mentality by focusing on "felt needs" and the healing of emotional "wounds." However, victimization shifts the attention away from one's own responsibility for what is thought, said, and done; away from one's own sin; and onto the sins of others committed against them. Victimization diverts believers away from the cross of Christ and their new life in Him.

> Therefore if any man be in Christ, he is a new creature: old things are passed away, behold, all things are become new (2 Cor. 5:17).

Victimization robs them of gratitude for God's unspeakable gift and thereby robs them of a close walk with Him.

Turning Christians into victims weakens their faith, stunts spiritual growth, and distorts their calling.

> For this is thankworthy, if a man for conscience toward God endure grief, suffering wrongfully.... if when ye do well, and suffer for it, ye take it patiently, this is acceptable with God. For even hereunto were ye called: because Christ also suffered for us, leaving us an example, that ye should follow his steps (1 Peter 2:19-21).

Every choice to walk according to the Spirit by grace through faith brings spiritual maturity. The choice is up to every believer, whether to be a psychologically defined and created victim or to be a biblically defined sinner saved by grace, walking according to the Spirit, and growing in the likeness of Christ.

11. Dishonoring Father and Mother

Dishonoring father and mother often occurs in problem-centered biblical counseling. When looking for the source of problems in a person's upbringing, problem-centered counseling often leads a person to violate God's commandment to: "Honour thy father and thy mother: that thy days may be long upon the land which the LORD thy God giveth thee" (Exod. 20:12). Even if a person is having problems related to parents, the principle to honor father and mother, repeated in Ephesians 6:2, is to be followed. This would mean not dishonoring mother and father to a "third party," especially when the parents are not there to respond (Proverbs 18:17). Contrary to Scripture, individuals are permitted and sometimes encouraged by the biblical counselor to talk about their past and present problems perceived to be related to parents (Exodus 20:12), and the counselee may carry on unrestrained by the counselor. Any counseling that opens the door to a person bad-mouthing parents leads to violating the Scriptural admonition to honor parents.

Much problem-centered counseling seeks to discover reasons for present problems in the past, and much time is devoted to insignificant details about how parents might have been over-protective or not protective enough, or how they might have smothered the child with too much love or not loved enough, or how the parents did this or that. Since no parent is perfect, this is fertile ground for a great deal of sinful communication. Such counseling also distorts a person's relationship with parents, because as negative things are discussed the positive things fade away until the adult child develops a strained relationship with the parents. In fact, some people, after this kind of counseling, divorce themselves completely from their parents. Problem-centered counseling has done a great disservice to parents, who are often blamed for nearly everything that is wrong in a person's life. This in itself violates the commandment to honor parents.

Not only do problem-centered counselors often permit their counselees to dishonor their mothers and fathers, they often encourage and participate in the process. Those who follow the Freudian formula will dishonor their mothers and fathers by blaming them for their current problems. It is sinful to do so.

Christ-centered helpers do not need to talk about a fellow believer's mother and father, but will encourage the direction away from parental blame and towards a focus on growing spiritually in the likeness of Christ. Jesus, the Word of God, and the work of the Holy Spirit will be the emphasis. After all, every true believer has been born again and has a new Father, a new life, a new family, and the indwelling Holy Spirit.

12. Women in Problem-Centered Counseling

From the very beginning of the talk therapy movement after World War II, the statistics always favored the preponderance of women in counseling over men. While more men are now entering counseling, the latest figures stand at two-thirds women and one-third men. Women enter counseling because they are attracted to it as a means of solving problems. Professional therapists in America are predominantly women. Members of the National Association of Marriage and Family Therapists are at least two-thirds women and the number of women clinical psychologists is catching up. Psychology ads for training counselors and ads for needed counseling or recovery are aimed primarily at women. Women's pictures are in almost all the ads.

Biblical counselors encourage women to do what they do so well—being verbal, nurturing, and relational. Women tend to share and converse. Medical doctor Louann Brizendine, in her book *The Female Brain*, describes a woman as "a person whose reality dictated that communication, connection, emotional sensitivity, and responsiveness were the primary values."[41] Brizendine's theme throughout the book is that women are different because they have different brains, and, as a result, women are deeply sensitive to emotions and form strong relationships. According to some theories, men in general are "better at systemizing" and "women are better at empathizing."[42] This expands the possibilities of sinful communication, especially when encouraged by problem-centered counselors. In the manner in which they function, biblical counselors appeal to women to come for help. The counselors, especially women, offer an environment for relationship and for exploring and expressing emotions in a conversational, female-friendly setting that suits women's feeling-oriented inclination to share. Counseling also provides an environment in which that strength can be corrupted.

Those who minister to women need to be aware of this strength that can be a great asset as long as they stay away from problem-centered counseling. Women need to be encouraged to find help if needed, but they should **not** be encouraged to become involved in problem-centered counseling that goes beyond biblical boundaries.

13. Men in Problem-Centered Counseling

The evidence is in. **Counseling is a functional environment for women and a dysfunctional environment for men**. While most men would naturally avoid it, they are often compelled to become involved. Once men become involved, their spiritual headship (Eph. 5) is easily and often usurped by the biblical counselor. Men on the whole are either not that interested in going to counseling or they are repelled by the whole idea of it.

Psychology Today discussed this topic in an article titled "Man's Last Stand: What Does It Take to Get a Guy into Therapy?" Regarding men seeking therapy, the article says:

> More often than not, the impetus is a woman. A typical male patient has been sent—usually by his wife, girlfriend or children, sometimes by his employer. Behind the command performance is a threat: "You change, or it's all over."[43]

One author-therapist, Terrence Real, refers to these as "wife mandated referrals." He says that the average man is unlikely to ask for counseling, because men do not consider therapy to be "manly."[44]

Of the total of those in counseling, the men who enter voluntarily are small in number. Gary Brooks, in his book *A New Psychotherapy for Traditional Men*, says, "Traditional men hate psychotherapy and will do most anything to avoid a therapist's office." He continues, "In fact, I believe that men's aversion to therapy is so powerful that it's wise to assume that most male clients, at some level, don't want to be there."[45]

As much as men are not attracted to counseling, virtually all avenues in and out of the church force them into it. Again, counseling is a female-friendly activity, which obtains male clients mostly through intimidation, exaggerated claims, expectations of others, or coercion. Behind most men in therapy is a woman, a court, an employer, a church denomination, or, as we have demonstrated elsewhere, a mission agency.[46]

Many biblical counselors rarely recognize the reluctance of men to be in problem-centered counseling and thus corrupt their biblical headship. The fact of a man often being coerced into counseling is not to suggest that a woman is the sole reason for it, but rather to say that she is a major reason. We conclude that, without a woman behind getting a man into therapy, the psychological and biblical counseling movements would be damaged, since up to one-third of the clients (men) could be affected. Moreover, if the other cultural, promotional, and legal incentives and mandates towards counseling were removed, most men on their own would avoid it all together.

Counselors of men and couples often mishandle Scripture by placing men in the problem-centered counseling setting, contrary to their spiritual headship. Men are often robbed of their biblical headship in the counseling room and also too often in the church. When a third party exercises the authoritative role of counseling, that person usurps the authority of the husband. Men should, of course, submit themselves, when necessary, to the discipline of their church or fellowship, but refuse the problem-centered biblical counselor's office. If help is needed, a man should seek those men who are mature in the faith and ignore biblical degrees or credentials. **If women are not in counseling as counselees, the men will not be there and the whole problem-centered counseling mania will disintegrate.**

14. A Man Counseling a Woman or Married Couple

In problem-centered counseling, when a man counsels a married woman or couple, there is a danger that he will displace the husband's spiritual headship in at least some measure, whether or not the husband is present. The types of problems a woman brings to a biblical counselor are often those that should be discussed with her husband, or, if not married and at home, with her father, mother or a more mature woman (Titus 2:3-5). **How many biblical counselors even think to ask the husband's consent to counsel his wife or a father's consent to counsel his dependent children?** And, how many biblical counselors know whether the husband or father has agreed to such counseling?

Oftentimes a wife will enter problem-centered counseling without her husband because of his reluctance, but this is also contrary to the headship given to men, because the counselor now functions in place of the husband. If the counselor is a man, he probably spends more time listening to other men's wives than to his own. What's worse is that the husband of the woman being counseled often comes off as second rate, because the male counselor spends time listening to the husband's wife in a contrived setting, in which he can appear extremely attentive and focused on her. In contrast, the husband may not appear as attentive and focused on her in the midst of their real life situations. Moreover, too many temptations occur in such counseling circumstances and many divorces have occurred because of them. Also, any talk about the husband in his absence (Prov. 18:17) is too often talebearing (Prov. 11:13; 18:8; 20:19; 26:20, 22) and even if true diminishes the husband's headship.

Another tragic result of a man counseling a woman is the fact that, absent the reality of the home environment of the woman, the counselor can misdirect the woman's loyalty and submission away from her husband or father, which can result in the counselor usurping the husband's or father's headship. Considering the above concerns, men should **not** be counseling women.

15. A Woman Counseling a Man or Married Couple

In problem-centered counseling, a woman counseling a man or a couple often erodes the biblical role of men and reduces or usurps his spiritual headship. It is difficult to counsel someone without having a spiritual headship role in the relationship. Biblical counseling is a spiritual setting; there will be doctrinal teaching and it is easy for a woman to usurp authority over a man in such a problem-centered environment, where biblical suggestions are made, spiritual directions given, and Bible study homework assigned. It is interesting to see those denominations and churches that would not permit a woman to preach in their pulpits nonetheless refer men to female problem-centered counselors, who by the very nature of counseling wield authority in spiritual matters.

The reverse of a man counseling a woman, as we discussed, can occur where the woman counselor can appear extremely attentive and focused on him. In contrast, the wife may not appear as attentive and focused on him in the midst of their real life situations. Moreover, too many temptations occur in such counseling circumstances and many divorces have occurred because of them. Also, any talk about the wife in her absence (Proverbs 18:17) is often talebearing (Prov. 11:13; 18:8; 20:19; 26:20, 22) and even if true diminishes the one-flesh principle.

16. One Up / One Down

The one-up/one-down relationship mentioned earlier is clearly unbiblical, but often maintained by many biblical counselors. The one-up/one-down relationship is a common result of all the emphasis on the certificated, degreed biblical counselor in contrast to mutual care in the Body of Christ (Gal. 6:1). Prior to the rise of the psychological counseling movement there were no biblical counseling certificates, degrees, or training levels. One medical doctor friend responded to this one-up/one-down relationship by saying, "That evil counselor-counselee (expert-dummy) relationship makes fools out of both, but few seem to see it."[47] Those who minister must do so with a spirit of meekness and of being alongside (not over).

> Brethren, if a man be overtaken in a fault, ye which are spiritual, restore such an one in the spirit of meekness; considering thyself, lest thou also be tempted. Bear ye one another's burdens, and so fulfil the law of Christ. For if a man think himself to be something, when he is nothing, he deceiveth himself (Gal. 6:1-3).

A pastor friend once said regarding ministering to others: **"One should have a recognition that we are but earthen vessels, simple, useless pots, that the glory and power is God's and not ours."** This should be a sobering reminder as to how one should minister to others.

17. One Week / One Month / One Year after Another

A number of Christians go to biblical counselors week after week, month after month, and some even year after year. Problem-centered counseling often encourages such long-term dependent relationships. There is no example in Scripture for such long-term counseling. We should have long-term relationships in the fellowship of the saints, but not in the biblical counselor's office. **Long-term relationships in counseling lead to long-term dependency.** Believers are to be dependent on the Lord and fulfill their own responsibilities within that relationship. "But let every man prove his own work, and then shall he have rejoicing in himself alone, and not in another. For every man shall bear his own burden" (Gal. 6:4, 5). The sooner every man bears his own burdens the better. The less problem-centered the counseling, the more dependency on the Word of God, the work of the Holy Spirit, and the fellowship of the saints, and the less dependency on the counselor.

18. Integration

Based on reading the books and articles by biblical counselors, listening to their talks, and asking them directly, we conclude that many biblical counselors are integrationists in that they integrate secular psychological theories and therapies with the Bible. We give several examples of this in our book *Against "Biblical Counseling": For the Bible*.[48] Some biblical counselors integrate psychological ideas,[49] others "recycle" psychological ideas,[50] and still others use material from integrationists, such as Dr. James Dobson and Dr. Larry Crabb, and integrationist organizations, such as the American Association of Christian Counselors.

Those who minister biblically must use the means that the Lord has given in His sufficient Word, in His Holy Spirit, and in the fellowship of the saints rather than integrate psychological ideas or use the works of those Christians who are integrationists.

19. Separated-from-the-Church Biblical Counseling Centers

Prior to the rise of the biblical counseling movement, which followed on the heels of the psychological counseling movement, there were no separated-from-the-church biblical counseling centers. No one was sent from a church for counseling because there was nowhere to send them. We trace the history of the cure of souls in *Against "Biblical Counseling": For the Bible*[51] and find at no time was there a referral out from the church to a separated-from-the-church center for personal care. Such ministry is a clear responsibility of the local church.

Referring individuals out of the church to a separated-from-the-church center to accomplish what the Lord has empowered His people to do in the local fellowship is a travesty on the teachings of the Bible and a failure on the part of the local fellowship. Yet, there are hundreds, if not thousands, of these separated-from-the-church counseling centers across America. There is no possibility in such a community center (which charges a fee) for ministering to people in the same way as in a local body of believers. There is no ministry beyond the 50-minute hour, no possibility to involve others as in a church fellowship, and no possibility for church discipline.

The local church is the place for pastoral care and the mutual edification of all believers, under the authority of the foundation laid by Scripture and as given by Jesus Christ within the mutual ministry of the saints one to another, for the purpose of building up the Body of Christ through mutual encouragement, admonition, confession, repentance, forgiveness, restoration, consolation, and comfort.

20. Charging Fees or Expecting Donations for Biblical Counseling

Charging fees or expecting donations for counseling is totally unbiblical and those biblical counselors who do so should be taken to task. Any such predators on Christians who are suffering problems of living and crying out for help should be put out of business. And, that's what it is! A ministry turned into a business to produce an income for the counselor at the expense and disadvantage of the person being counseled.

The fastest way to put a stop to this outrage against Scripture and biblical church practice is for church leaders to speak out against such money extracting practices. **For how many more years will church leaders hear so-called biblical counselors close in prayer and ask, "Will you pay by cash, check, or credit card?" before utterly condemning such a recent, never-heard-of-before church practice?**

Scripture does not support charging a fee or expecting a donation for biblical counseling. We have written a number of articles revealing how sinful it is to charge for biblical counseling.[52] The most often quoted verse to support charging is Luke 10:7 ". . . for the labourer is worthy of his hire." The dictionary definition of *hire* is "to engage the services of a person for wages."[53] The person who does the hiring is the one to set the wages. But those who use the verse believe the following: "Since the labourer is worthy of his hire he can charge," which contradicts who sets the wages (the one who employs) and who sets the amount (the one who employs). In other words, the counselee selects and engages the laborer (the counselor) and therefore should set the amount of wages to be paid. In addition, the Greek word for *hire* in Luke 10:7 is a noun. *Vine's* gives two possible English words for the Greek as *hire* or *wages*.[54] In other words, Luke 10:7 could be translated as "the labourer is worthy of his wages." If one uses the word *wages*, it is still true that the employer (counselee) sets the wages and not the one providing the labor (counselor).

Yes, "the labourer is worthy of his hire" (Luke 10:7), and "the labourer is worthy of his reward" (1 Timothy 5:18). Paul even argued that as he had sown spiritual things, should he not also reap carnal things (1 Corinthians 9:11). Nevertheless, he also said: "What is my reward then? Verily that, when I preach the gospel, I may make the gospel of Christ **without charge,** that I abuse not my power in the gospel" (1 Corinthians 9:18). Peter wrote to the elders: "Feed the flock of God which is among you, taking the oversight thereof, not by constraint, but willingly; **not for filthy lucre,** but of a ready mind" (1 Peter 5:2).

If we use the twisted application of Luke 10:7 and apply it throughout the church to those who labor, it will justify charges for pastoral visits to homes and hospitals, church services, communion, etc. Some will protest that a pastor is already paid and thus cannot charge. However, think about all the other services of those who labor in the church, such as deacons, elders, and the many others who teach, lead, and work. In some churches this would amount to hundreds of hours; in other churches it would total thousands of hours. Using the same Luke 10:7 rationale as the biblical counselors who charge, these people who volunteer numerous hours could charge as well. Even if they are paid, it should be according to Luke 10:7, that is: the church sets the wages and not the individuals who labor, as would be the case if one applied the erroneous twisting of Luke 10:7.

One of the more egregious examples of "for the labourer is worthy of his hire" was reported in a *Charisma* magazine article, which told about a New York City pastor who has been "charging $365 for personal prophecies." The article says, "Self-proclaimed prophet E. Bernard Jordan says he has a word from God for those who are struggling to find direction in life. But, unlike biblical prophets who offered their counsel for free, Jordan's messages sometimes come with a $365 price tag."[55] This is obviously outrageous in many respects, but the amount of money is probably a lot less than many biblical counselors receive from a single counselee for their ministry.

The dictionary definition of a *client* involves the use of professional advice or services from a person or group.[56] The dictionary definition of a *professional* is one "following an occupation as a means of livelihood or for gain."[57] **So technically speaking, the biblical counselors who charge should be referred to as "professional counselors" and their counselees should be called "clients."** However, because this sounds so crass, the biblical counselors avoid these terms entirely.

Whether one agrees with biblical counseling or not, it is a ministry. It is designed to minister the Word of God empowered by the Holy Spirit by one who knows Christ to one who will receive it. It is sinful to require a charge for such a ministry. There is no example in Scripture that justifies charging a fee for ministering the Word of God by the grace of God to a brother or sister in Christ. Again, someone might protest that a minister is paid a salary. But that is a false analogy. The true analogy would be charging someone a fee to attend church. We hope no one would even think of doing that!

This pay for service makes such biblical counseling sinful. Imagine someone going to a biblical counseling center for ministry concerning a life issue? Let's say that the conversation and direction are biblical. Can you imagine at the end a prayer, an Amen, and then a bill for services? Would

Paul or the disciples have done such a thing? Absolutely not!

Simoniacs?

A *simoniac* is "a person who practices simony," and *simony* is "the buying or selling of sacred or spiritual things." Charging fees for counseling is one example of charging for a church ministry. Another example of simony is the sale of indulgences in the Roman Catholic church. The Catholic church was selling and people thought they were buying their way to heaven.

Filthy lucre (1 Peter 5:2) is the great financial fuel that drives the psychological counseling movement and some-times even the biblical counseling movement. Without the charging of fees or the hope of receiving payments in the future for those being trained, the biblical counseling move-ment would be seriously affected.

No one knows how much is received annually by all the so-called biblical counselors in or out of churches across America. It is obviously a huge sum of money. The direct charging and receiving of money for personal ministry is just one of many factors in which biblical counselors parrot psychological counselors. **It is a disgrace and a shame for the church to sit silently and permit such a blight to exist in her midst.**

The content and controlling factor of Christian counsel-ing should be the sacred Word of God:

> According as his divine power hath given unto us all things that pertain unto life and godliness, through the knowledge of him that hath called us to glory and virtue: Whereby are given unto us exceeding great and precious promises: that by these ye might be partakers of the divine nature, having escaped the

corruption that is in the world through lust (2 Peter 1:3,4).

True biblical counsel involves the Word of God and the work of the Holy Spirit, sometimes directly to a person, but sometimes through another who knows Christ as Savior, ministered to one who receives it for deliverance and change. **True Christian ministry or the cure of souls is a sacred, spiritual work done by God, not man. It is a ministry to give; not to sell!**

Consider men and women whose lives are affected by fears, anxieties, depression, marital conflicts, family conflicts, or any one of a number of other traumas of life, some by virtue of their own sins and others by virtue of the sins of others, to be ministered the wisdom and grace of God and then to be told that they must pay for such ministry! **Can you imagine Jesus or His disciples praying for souls in such jeopardy and then saying, "Cash, check or credit card"? It boggles the imagination!**

In conclusion, the hirer sets the wages and not the laborer. The biblical counselors who charge are in grave biblical error. There are numerous other biblical reasons not to charge, which we discuss in our previous writings.[58] We say to those many who call themselves "biblical counselors" and who extract fees or even suggest donations for such ministry: **Repent of this sinful wickedness and ask God for forgiveness!** And, we exhort those organizations that train individuals to counsel to speak out strongly against such an evil practice instead of justifying its existence.

As many writers throughout the centuries have said, Simon the sorcerer no doubt wished to sell what he wanted to buy from the disciples. Deborah J. Dewart, Attorney at Law and seminary graduate, has written an excellent theological evaluation of this issue titled "Charging Fees for Biblical Counseling? Relationship, Responsibility, and Remuneration."[59] We add one final warning: charging for biblical counseling opens the door for lawsuits.

21. What Not To Do Conclusion

Eliminating talebearing, talking about others not present, blaming the past, playing the victim, dishonoring mother and father, as well as other sinful conversations, from counseling could lead to a true restoration of the cure of souls and a Christ-centered ministry of mutual care among believers. **Christians should stay out of problem-centered counseling.** As we often say, the ongoing problem-centeredness of biblical counselors is not supported in Scripture, neither are the types of conversations about problems, as seen in the biblical counseling case studies, supported by Scripture. **Probably the best way to expose the sinful nature of problem-centered counseling is to read anecdotes and case studies using the biblical standards discussed here.** Because of all the previous reasons, we do not recommend any of the biblical counseling organizations, books, programs, certificates, or degrees. **We challenge leaders in the BCM to demonstrate that they counsel without violating the preceding sinful practices.** If just the sinful practices discussed here were corrected by the problem-centered biblical counselors, that would be the end of the BCM. However, that could be the beginning of a true biblical, Christ-centered ministry.

The biblical counseling movement as it currently exists must die. Is there any hope for the biblical counseling movement? Yes, but only resurrected in its proper place as a part of the biblically ordained ministries of the church.

In this Part One, we presented **What Not to Do** as a means of clearing the church of the many unbiblical teachings that are practiced in the BCM, so that those who desire to minister biblically will know **What Not to Do**. In Part Two we indicate **What to Avoid** by critiquing the nouthethic and the idols-of-the-heart counseling approaches, which are probably the best known of the BCM systems, and reveal that, while well known and much used, they are nonetheless **not** truly as biblical as claimed. In Part Three we indicate **What Can Be Done** as a confirmation to those who are already ministering and as an encouragement to those who are spiritually ready but have been reluctant to do so.

PART TWO

What to Avoid

Problem-Centered "Biblical" Counseling

22. Introduction

There is some good biblical material in the various manuals, books, and certificate and degree programs. However, one major undoing of the biblical counseling movement (BCM) is found in their anecdotes and case studies. It is their Achilles heel! **The good biblical material is undone by their cases, which reveal what they actually do.** However, many of these books are totally absent of the conversation and dialogues that typically go on in biblical counseling. There are thousands of biblical counseling books, tapes, and conferences, but **not many have literal case studies with detailed dialogue. Probably the best way to expose the unbiblical nature of problem-centered biblical counseling is to read available anecdotes and case studies, using the biblical standards, some of which are discussed in Part One.** There one can check out how the counseling problems are discussed and what conversations are involved. They are heavily problem-centered in the most unbiblical ways and often involve evil speaking.

In the following we give two examples of problem-centered counseling. The first one is working on the outside (nouthetic counseling) and the second one is working on the inside (idols-of-the-heart counseling). *The Case of the "Hopeless" Marriage* is a quintessential example of nouthetic counseling, originated by Dr. Jay Adams, and Dr. David Powlison's "idols-of-the-heart" case is a quintessential example of the working-on-the-inside counseling.

We begin by quoting Adams with respect to public criticism in the church. He says:

> Any Christian who sets himself up as a teacher in the church of Christ and publicly teaches anything thereby opens himself up for criticism by others (cf. James 3:1). If they think what he is teaching is harmful to the church, they have an obligation to point it out just as widely as it was taught. Such public warning or debate on a topic should not be considered a personal attack at all.... What a critic of a public teaching does in pointing out his disagreement with that teaching has nothing to do with personal affronts or lack of reconciliation; he is simply disagreeing at the same public level as that on which the teaching was given in the first place.[1]

23. Case Studies

Case studies are often used in psychological and biblical counseling to show forth the usefulness of a particular idea or methodology. Aside from using brief examples to illustrate a point, we are opposed to the use of case studies for a variety of reasons. In our reading of psychological counseling case studies over the years, we see a greater honesty with respect to open discussion of cases that failed. We have seen none of these discussed in the biblical counseling movement, and not because they are not there. As we said earlier, one of the many reasons we left the biblical counseling movement is because there is little or no authentic self-examination in the movement.

Drs. Elizabeth Loftus and Melvin Guyer wrote a two-part article with the subtitle "The Hazards of the Single Case History." They began by saying:

> Case histories have a long and cherished tradition in science. They are compelling anecdotes, often powerful enough to generate entire theories of behavior. Freud built the edifice of psychoanalytic theory on the very few cases he saw in therapy. Bruno Bettelheim used a few cases of autistic children to conclude that autism is caused by "refrigerator" mothers. Psychiatrist Cornelia Wilbur's account of her patient, "Sybil," captivated millions of people who believed the story of Sybil's "multiple personalities."[2]

All of these theories, based on "very few cases," have been powerfully influential in the practice of psychotherapists; but **all have been debunked**. Loftus and Guyer say:

> But case studies, by definition, are bounded by the perceptions and interpretations of the storyteller. If they are well told . . . readers often find them far more persuasive and compelling than the stodgy numbers and cautions of science.[3]

Dr. Paul Meehl, a past president of the American Psychological Association, once wrote an extensive paper as to "Why I Do Not Attend Case Conferences," in which he indicates a multitude of reasons for his concerns. [4] Many biblical counselors use anecdotal case studies throughout their books, manuals, and conferences, and many of the same objections apply. In one instance the biblical counselor used a case of a person whom he had never met, but had only heard about from a third party. Caution: while brief examples may be all right, one should not be intimidated by these biblical counseling cases that prove an approach or point of view of the biblical counselor or are used to demonstrate how to counsel, whether presented in writing or given verbally at conferences. We give two such examples here in Part Two.

It is time for Christians to give up trying to learn how to counsel by studying or listening to anecdotes and cases. In addition to other reasons given above, anecdotes and case studies can get in the way. Two people could have exactly the same external problem, but only God knows the specifics of what and how for a particular person. That is why we say that those who minister to one another need to get **in** the way but **out** of the way. They need to be available, but they need to let God work rather than push their own agenda or employ methods and techniques championed by some self-styled human "expert."

These cautions apply to all counseling cases. If we were presenting a case, it would be easy enough to put words in the mouth of our fictional counselor and create composite responses and dialog on the part of the fictional counselees with their fictional pastor. Anyone who has counseled for a period of time could contrive a composite case to prove the value of what is done. Each one could take a very different approach from Adams and Powlison and present a contrived composite case with equally difficult challenges and a happy ending. All who claim to be biblical counselors, no matter how different from or how contradictory to nouthetic and idols-of-the-heart counseling, could contrive a composite case to "prove" whatever they wish, especially if they are gifted story tellers. **The variety of biblical counseling approaches should be judged not even on the use of**

Bible verses, but rather on whether or not they are truly biblical approaches.

As one reads the anecdotes and case studies and descriptions, one may become impressed with how erudite and facile the counselors appear to be, but one does not need to be erudite or facile in analyzing others. Instead, one needs to be biblical, not analytical. In fact, the more erudite and facile sounding one is the less truly biblical one is likely to be. Additionally, if it sounds esoteric rather than biblically clear, it is likely to be untrustworthy.

24. Counselor, Counselee, Counseling

As we established earlier, using the designations *counselor*, *counselee*, and *counseling* as those in the biblical counseling movement use them is not biblically supportable.[5] All three terms are used throughout nouthetic and idols-of-the-heart counseling. In contrast, we refer to what we do as biblical ministry, as others have done prior to the rise of the psychological and biblical counseling movements. The biblical counseling movement has turned biblical ministry into biblical counseling, but there is no biblical justification for the biblical counseling movement as practiced today.

We challenge all biblical counselors to demonstrate exegetically from Scripture that the use of the Hebrew and Greek words for *counsel, counsels counselled, counseller, counsellers*, and *counsellor* in the Old and New Testaments are anything like what occurs in nouthetic and idols-of-the-heart counseling. (See Part One and Appendices A and B.) Nowhere in the Old Testament or the New Testament does one find counseling in the manner typically described in biblical counseling. Those who minister biblically should not use such terms.[6] We only use these terms in critiquing those who use them to describe what they do.

25. NANC
Nouthetic Counseling

The Case of the "Hopeless" Marriage (hereafter, *The Case*) is authored by Dr. Jay E. Adams.[7] *The Case* is the *ne plus ultra* of nouthetic counseling. It is a perfect example of the nouthetic counseling approach, which was originated by Adams. Therefore, all who are trained to counsel nouthetically should desire to emulate this example, and all who train others in the nouthetic approach should hold up *The Case* as the epitome of what to copy.

The subtitle of *The Case* explains the contents: *A Nouthetic Counseling Case from Beginning to End.* The cover indicates that the book was written "with Greg Dawson [pastor] and Bert and Sue Lancaster [counselees]." We believe the coauthorship is probably just poetic license and that *The Case* was written solely by Adams, who says: "All names and places in this book are likewise fictional and apply to no known persons walking on the face of the earth" (p. 2). According to Adams, *The Case* "is a composite based upon a number of those in which, over the years, I have counseled husbands and wives about marriages" (p. 1). However, at the conclusion of the counseling Pastor Greg asks Bert and Sue, "Would you give permission for me to write up our counseling sessions as they have occurred in a book designed to help others learn what goes on behind closed counseling doors?" (p. 135). The couple agrees to have their case written up in a book.

So which is it, a contrived composite case to show a practical example of how nouthetic counseling is conducted or an actual case hidden with anonymous names or fiction through and through? In spite of the possibility that it is a real case, but disguised, we conclude that it is more likely a composite case as Adams says. There is also much internal evidence of this being a **contrived composite** case than evidence for it being real. The dialog and progression from the beginning of the case to the end are all too predictable and tailored to a happy conclusion. *The Case* fits the old adage, "If it sounds too good to be true, it probably is." Like Sigmund Freud himself, any psychological or biblical counselor with any experience could write a case to support whatever psychological or biblical approach they use and have a similar happy ending. And, as you read their cases, it is obvious that many have.

Adams says, "Having counseled two hours a day, two days a week, for several years, I think that I can fairly exhibit the sorts of things that husbands and wives do and say, as well as how counselors must respond" (p. 1). We approach this evaluation of *The Case* from similar experience, as we have been biblically ministering to individuals, couples, and families for over thirty years and have trained others to do likewise. For a number of years we headed what we called at the time "biblical counseling" at a church (we now refer to what we do and did as biblical ministry) and we have taught many to minister through classes, books we have written, correspondence, and presentations. Many others who do not use the nouthetic approach have some of the same practical experiences. **However, the true test is not personal experience, but whether or not nouthetic counseling or any other approach is truly biblical, not how many hours one has counseled or how many books one has written or how many degrees one has earned.**

26. Nouthetic Fundamentals

A couple, Bert and Sue, are being counseled by Pastor Greg. There are ten sessions of counseling and we select from some of the remarks made by them. Adams has Pastor Greg say the following:

> Many—perhaps most—of those who call their counseling "Christian" or even "biblical" don't really counsel according to the Scriptures.... Truly biblical counseling, in contrast, grows out of and is consistent with the Scriptures **at every point** (p. 118, bold added).

The following critique of *The Case of the "Hopeless" Marriage: A Nouthetic Counseling Case from Beginning to End* will demonstrate that **nouthetic counseling is not truly biblical "at every point."** *The Case* has a biblical façade and has a biblical intent but is not truly biblical "**at every point.**" In fact, some of *The Case* may reveal Adams' particular brand of Presbyterianism rather than being truly biblical.

Throughout the nouthetic counseling case, Adams comments on the progress. After a brief interchange between Pastor Greg and the couple during the first session, Adams says:

> It looks, then, as if Greg is on track since he has begun to do the three most fundamental things that a counselor should work on in the first session: **basic data gathering, giving a reason to hope, setting the rules for counseling** (pp. 9-10, bold added).

The "**basic data gathering**" refers to Pastor Greg's use of the Personal Data Inventory (PDI), which we will discredit shortly.

"**Giving a reason to hope**" refers to Pastor Greg's following comments:

I want you to know that I'll **work with you for as long as necessary to help you solve your problems**. And—let me say at the outset—they *can* be solved. I say that because you're both Christians. That means that you have newness of life to enable you to do God's will, you have the Bible to direct you how to do it, and you have God's Spirit to strengthen and help you do it (p. 7, italics in original, bold added).

Following this, Pastor Greg says:

Now, let me explain a few things. I've already said that as Christians it's always possible to solve problems if you are willing to do so. But that's true only *if* you follow God's directions in His Word. No matter how bad the marriage is right now, **I *guarantee* that God will give you a marriage that sings, if you follow His directions!** But it *will* take doing what He says. I can say this because God has promised that (p. 8, italics in original, bold added).

Pastor Greg's promise to **"work with you for as long as necessary to help you solve your problems"** gives a false hope to the couple. What if it takes years? What if no progress is being made? What if the marriage gets worse and they file for divorce?

Another false hope is in Pastor Greg's statement: **"I *guarantee* that God will give you a marriage that sings, if you follow His directions!"** Even if they follow God at every point, further trials and tragedies may come that God will enable them to endure, but the idea of **"a marriage that sings"** is too focused on temporal enjoyment and too dependent on circumstances. Biblically speaking, what is **"a marriage that sings"**? The call of a Christian couple is not to have **"a marriage that sings"** for their mutual enjoyment, but a marriage that reflects Christ and His church (Ephesians 5).

The third most fundamental item in nouthetic counseling is "**setting the rules for counseling**." We comment on this later as we reveal the unbiblical result of one of Pastor Greg's rules for communication.

These "three most fundamental things that a counselor should work on in the first session" according to the nouthetic way are all riddled with faults. As we discuss shortly: there is no biblical need for the PDI; there is no biblical need to inject hope in the manner done by Pastor Greg; and there is no biblical justification for communication rules that allow and even foster sinful communication.

27. Personal Data Inventory

Adams begins the case with Bert and Sue completing the Personal Data Inventory (PDI). The PDI requires one to list "Identification Data" (Personal), "Health Information," and "Marriage and Family Information." At the end of the PDI are six questions. At the beginning of the case, Adams presents four of the PDI questions with Bert and Sue's answers.

Prior to the creation and use of the PDI Christians did minister to one another and they were in no way hampered or restricted by the non-use of the PDI. Actually using the PDI could subtract from, rather than add to, the counseling process, because it will often provide distractions from the real need and it is totally unnecessary.

Pastor Greg will not only use Bert and Sue's PDI answers to guide his counseling, but he will also exercise guesses, assumptions, and opinions regarding why they answered the way they did. Adams discusses Bert and Sue's answers on the PDI. He raises questions prompted by Bert and Sue's answers that lead to guessing. For instance, Adams says:

> Note the brevity of Bert's answers. Is he embarrassed? Does he really care about the marriage—about Sue? ... In response to question #2, he opens up a bit. It seems that he might want to preserve the marriage, but hasn't the faintest idea what to do....
>
> In contrast, look at Sue's more detailed responses. If she thinks there's no hope, why is she here? ... Does she agree with the psychologist? She didn't take his advice, yet keeps on mentioning what he said. She probably got the idea of "incompatibility" from him....
>
> Greg is thinking well about what he read. He has used their answers productively to stimulate his thinking. He probably scribbled some of his tentative thoughts on his *Weekly Counseling Record* [a form in Adams' book *The Christian Counselor's Manual* to be used for recording counseling notes] (p. 5).

This kind of guessing and presuming are characteristic of biblical counseling and would be absent in true biblical ministry as there is no need for it. Adams is wise in not including what Pastor Greg wrote into his notes, because there would no doubt be more obvious assumptions and opinions along with the questions that lead to guessing. Much guesswork goes on in problem-centered counseling. Besides being entirely inappropriate, it has no biblical basis.

Adams says, "Note the brevity of Bert's answers," on the PDI. Adams may not be aware of two important facts. First, men in general do not want to be in counseling.[8] Second, women have special characteristics[9]; they are more verbal and relational than men.[10] In other words the counseling environment is more female friendly. These two facts seem to be little known to those in the biblical counseling movement, but are irrelevant when one ministers to fellow believers without doing problem-centered counseling. Men do not naturally want to participate in problem-centered counseling; they are more open to Christ-centered ministry done biblically as it does not threaten their spiritual headship.

The PDI and other such inventories are considered to be valuable by problem-centered counselors, but can be a detriment when ministering biblically. Also, using the PDI is entirely unnecessary as thousands of individuals who call themselves biblical counselors and others who minister biblically have never used one and could contrive equally successful cases as the one manufactured by Adams.

28. Problem-Centered Nouthetic Counseling

Nouthetic counseling is a problem-centered counseling approach. **If there is no ongoing discussion of problems there is no counseling**. Therefore, those who counsel must have problems revealed, described, and discussed in order for counseling to take place. *The Case* is a perfect example of this. Nouthetic counselors and others in the biblical counseling movement depend upon knowing problems in detail and offering solutions. Bible verses used are related to the problems and homework is problem-centered. As Pastor Greg says: "The more I know [about the problem] the more I can help" (p. 41).

In reading *The Case*, one would think that the counselor with all his knowledge and training is the most important person in the counseling relationship. In fact, Adams poses the following near the beginning of the book: "Their marriage seems in *serious* danger at this point. If he [Pastor Greg] fails in his counseling, it will probably break up. We must await to see what he does" (emphasis his, p. 6). In other words, the success of this counseling rests significantly on the counselor. Pastor Greg's promise to work with Bert and Sue "as long as necessary to help [them] solve [their] problems" makes his role sound vital, almost as if their problems could not be solved without him. Not only is his importance exaggerated; Adams makes him sound like a real expert: "As always, Greg seems to know where he wants to go and will anticipate and lead them to those places **that breed confidence in him**" (p. 120, bold added). In fact, Pastor Greg even talks as though he can predict the future when he says of Bert's mother, "I predict that in time she'll come around" (p. 111).

As we mentioned earlier, scientific research evidence diminishes the importance of the counselor and the counselor's training, experience, and methods. According to the research, the most important human elements in change are Bert and Sue and their desire to change. Worse than that, Pastor Greg works to "**breed confidence in him**," that is, in himself. A truly biblical ministry would always be to encourage greater confidence in the Lord. This exaggerated importance of the counselor and his expertise reflects the theories and practices of secular psychotherapy, diminishes the role of the Holy Spirit, and discourages ordinary members of the Body of Christ from ministering to one another.

The assumption in *The Case* is that Bert and Sue are Christians, since they had "joined the 'First Scriptural Presbyterian Church' two years ago." Adams further says, "Both were converted under the evangelistic efforts of one of the church's elders" (p. 2). Pastor Greg also refers to them as "both Christians" (p. 7). However, the fact that Bert and Sue are members of the church is no guarantee that they are true believers. Sometimes it's helpful to ignore the fact that they are church members and ask about their relationship with the Lord. At other times whether or not they are saved will become apparent as one ministers in the direction we present later and in Part Three.

Bert and Sue come to Pastor Greg for help because their marriage is falling apart (p. 1). Bert and Sue describe their problems in the PDI and then Pastor Greg discusses their problems with them. He asks questions about the problems, because, as a nouthetic counselor, he must gather data about the problems, which is unnecessary when one is truly biblical.

The following are the types of problems surfaced by the couple (pp. 71, 105, 114):

Bert: Does not pick up his socks.
        Does not take out the trash regularly.
Sue: Unloads on Bert as soon as he comes home from work.
        Does not serve meals that please Bert.

When the pastor asks Bert to tell him about the main problem in their marriage, Bert replies, "Well, we haven't been getting along for some time now. It seems that she won't let me be the head of the house. I..." At that point Sue interrupts Bert and says, "Won't let you. When did you ever try? You know full well that you..." The pastor then interrupts Sue and asks her to let Bert finish what he was saying. Then Bert says, "Well, as I was saying—before she flew into one of her tirades..." Sue interrupts again and says, "See, pastor, he can't be civil. A tirade? Hummph!" (p. 11).

The pastor invites Bert to continue even though he is speaking ill about his wife and exposing her faults to a third party. Bert then says, "As I was saying, every time I try to assume my duty as the head of my home, Sue undermines me. She always knows better. She always has another way.

She always contradicts me. The kids don't know who to believe" (p. 12).

The pastor does set some restrictions on their rude and hurtful communication, such as having them speak to him instead of to each other and telling them not to exaggerate. Thus they are allowed to speak ill of one another as long as they do not speak directly to each other. Not being allowed to speak to one another during counseling is an artificial restriction that does not prevent the sinful talk, but merely keeps things somewhat under the pastor's control. He thereby maintains his authoritative position rather than being reduced to being on the sidelines during any argument that might erupt. One can easily see how the problem-centeredness of the counseling opens the door to couples breaking God's commandments to husbands and wives in Ephesians 5.

When the pastor attempts to teach Bert about loving his wife, he responds, "It's just that if she'd listen to me, I could love her more." Then when the pastor gives biblical instruction regarding the husband to love his wife, Sue remarks, "See, I told him! He should love me by putting me first" (p. 15). This evil talk could have been avoided if the pastor had cautioned them at the beginning about how speaking ill of one another and exposing each other's faults are the very opposite of love and respect.

At the end of the first session, Pastor Greg assigns homework. He says:

> Each of you is to compose a list of 100 or more ways that you are failing God as a person, as a husband or wife, and as a father or mother.... Write out your lists, and when you've finished draw a line and then hand the lists to one another to add anything that may be missing. **List specific things that bother you about one another** (p. 21, bold added).

This is a long list of 200 possible problems the couple has as "a person, as a husband or wife, and as a father or mother." Add this to problems already revealed in the PDI and the problems already discussed and the problem-centered counselor has the usual pile of problems to serve as fodder for future problem-centered counseling sessions. The mere listing of their gripes and failings could easily make matters worse. Listing 100 or more ways each for Bert and Sue is a negative and unnecessary assignment, but it does give the nouthetic counselor something to talk about for the upcoming sessions. In addition, we wonder how many couples would actually do the assignment and how many might not come back, but when one contrives a case, one can make the imaginary couple do anything.

It would have been far better to suggest to Bert and Sue that each one bring back a list of items for which they are thankful to the Lord. These can be a springboard away from problem-centeredness to Christ-centeredness. Moving them from their thanksgiving list to prayer, the Word, and worship would encourage them to grow spiritually, draw closer to the Lord, and thereby, in most cases, enable them to deal with their problems on their own. (See Part Three.)

While the pastor has given some good instruction along the way, the problem-centeredness of biblical counseling comes out again when Sue says to Bert, "You've never done much disciplining, Bert—I've had it all on my shoulders. You know that. Don't make it sound like you have!" In response, Bert says, "Now, Sue, you know how hard I've tried, but to be honest, you also know that you always contradict what I tell them [the children] and they get confused. In time, I finally gave up" (p. 75). Whoops! Here they are breaking the pastor's rule. They are speaking to each other here instead of complaining about each other to the pastor.

There is no biblical example in Scripture of the type of counseling as practiced in *The Case*. Such repeated airing of complaints about each other and ongoing discussions about problems of living during numerous counseling sessions as in *The Case* have no precedence in Scripture. This one-week-after-another, one-to-one or one-to-two in this case, one-appointment-after-another (p. 39), and the **one-up of Pastor Greg** are all part of the onerous ones referred to earlier.[11] The one-upmanship of Pastor Greg fits perfectly into our medical doctor friend's remark quoted earlier: "That evil counselor-counselee (expert-dummy) relationship makes fools out of both, but few seem to see it." Examples of this can be seen throughout *The Case*. In Galatians 6:1-3 the apostle Paul speaks of the necessary humility on the part of the one who ministers, which would abrogate the one-up/one-down approach of nouthetic counseling.

The Case gives the impression that it's as easy as falling off a log to transform a troubled marriage when in reality (as we have demonstrated earlier) it is probably one of the most difficult areas to deal with because of problem-centeredness.[12] There are biblical ways to deal with personal failings and sinfulness. For those who minister biblically, it is not necessary to know specifics about the problems or to always offer solutions directly related to the problems.

29. External Behavior

Nouthetic counseling invariably leads to working on external behavior (the "problem") and ends up being a program of works (do's and don't's). At the encouragement of Pastor Greg to prepare a list of ways that Bert could give himself to Sue (p. 55), Bert comes up with the following:

1. Fix broken vacuum cleaner handle.

2. Spend time with the kids on Saturday so Sue can be freed up.
3. Clear the table after meals.
4. Take Sue out for dinner once a month while having a baby sitter stay with the boys (p. 57).

Bert's list is a characteristic result of nouthetic counseling and other problem-centered approaches. The counselees are encouraged to write such lists and then encouraged to follow them. There is no precedence for this in the Bible or, for that matter, in the past history of ministry in the church. It is a result of following the practices of the secular psychological counseling movement, which is problem-centered. The do's and don't's and should's and ought's in *The Case* are heavily behaviorally oriented. Nouthetic counseling strongly emphasizes external behavior.

Adams trusts that as people change their external behavior, they will also change their attitudes and other aspects of their internal selves. He has Pastor Greg saying such things as this: "You know, Bert, great changes in attitudes can result from small changes in behavior" (p. 45). He repeats the same idea later: "You see, just as I said when discussing the socks, large changes in attitudes can take place over small changes in behavior" (p. 47). Consequently there is much teaching having to do with external behavior and rules to follow. For Adams, spiritual growth appears to be more dependent on what one **does** than on faith in Christ working **in** the believer.

Adams has been consistent in promoting this idea of external change leading to internal change. In his book *Competent to Counsel* he says, "God sets forth the important principle that behavior determines feelings.... People feel bad because of bad behavior; feelings flow from actions."[13] There appears to be far more emphasis on what one is to do in nouthetic counseling than on the very life of Christ in the believer.

Throughout his methodology, Adams has stressed changing behavior and habits as a means of inner change and spiritual growth. However, all the external change that Bert and Sue make could be done in the flesh just by believing that their circumstances would improve and they would have a "marriage that sings" if they made these small changes. While problems may be solved and people may develop new habits, there may be no true spiritual growth, even when an interest is being shown in knowing more of the Bible. The Pharisees were experts in Scripture and in external behavior as well.

Scripture teaches about believers working out (through obedience) what God is working in them "both to will and to do of his good pleasure" (Phil. 2:12, 13). However, Adams seems to reverse the order this way: as believers follow God's commandments on the outside, they are doing the work of God on the inside. Adams appears to be committed to the idea that righteousness comes from obeying the law, for he declares: "Liberty comes through the law, not apart from it."[14] The epistle to the Galatians teaches the opposite: "Stand fast therefore in the liberty wherewith Christ hath made us free, and be not entangled again with the yoke of bondage" (Gal. 5:1) and is confirmed in Romans:

> For the law of the Spirit of life in Christ Jesus hath made me free from the law of sin and death. For what the law could not do, in that it was weak through the flesh, God sending his own Son in the likeness of sinful flesh, and for sin, condemned sin in the flesh: That the righteousness of the law might be fulfilled in us, who walk not after the flesh, but after the Spirit (Romans 8:2-4).

Scripture clearly teaches that, though the law is holy and has great purposes and effects, it cannot make one holy. Not even the moral law can make one righteous. The believer who is living the new life in Christ will express the law of the Spirit through external obedience, but does not establish or even develop the inner life through the correction of external behavior. One becomes holy through what Christ has already accomplished and continues to work in the believer throughout the process of sanctification. The holiness comes from Christ. It is expressed through holy living, not the other way around. If one attempts to become holy by behavior, one merely cleans up the outside (Matt. 23:25), but if one becomes holy by faith in the finished work of Christ, the resulting change in behavior will be an expression of the holy life within.

Bert can be encouraged to pick up his socks or to pick up his Bible. Nouthetic counseling, while not ignoring the Bible would emphasize Bert picking up his socks, while biblical ministry would emphasize Bert picking up the Bible, without ignoring needed changes in his outward behavior.

30. Discussing Marital Problems

Bert and Sue argue, exhibit anger towards one another, and heap blame on one another all in Pastor Greg's presence. While he sets up rules for them not to speak directly to each other, he allows and even encourages them to talk about each other and to express their frustration with each other to him. He ends up being a kind of referee to enable them to talk about what's wrong with each other and to expose each other's failings so that he will have something to work with in this problem-centered environment.

As we have demonstrated earlier from Scripture, discussing marital problems in one another's presence to a third party is unbiblical.[15] Also, as discussed earlier, the problem-centered approach taken in nouthetic counseling tends to corrupt the biblical roles of both men and women, and particularly in marital counseling.[16] Pastor Greg corrupts Bert's spiritual headship by eliciting and discussing problems in the marriage and then leading the couple to solutions. Pastor Greg corrupts Sue's role by having her submit to himself rather than to her husband. Biblical ministry will encourage Bert and Sue to grow biblically and thus spiritually. (See Part Three) In that way Bert will learn to obey the Lord in exercising his spiritual headship in love, and Sue will learn to submit to Bert "as unto the Lord" (Eph. 5:22-33).

Pastor Greg's counseling encourages the couple to sin in order to save their marriage. Pastor Greg is in the process of "establishing rules: no interruptions, no **nasty** talk" (bold added), but "nasty talk" is already condoned and encouraged by Pastor Greg, who is only curbing against exaggeration and the two speaking directly to one another (pp. 11-13). Adams says: "You will notice that Pastor Greg has established God's Word as the standard for what will go on in counseling" (p. 13). Nevertheless, Pastor Greg has allowed and even encouraged through the PDI and subsequent conversation unedifying statements to be made by the couple about each other (see Eph. 4:29). There is murmuring, complaining, not showing love to the wife, and dishonoring the husband.

It is unfortunate and unbiblical that Pastor Greg in "establishing rules" says "no **nasty** talk." The word *nasty* is deplorable because the first definition of the word nasty is "physically filthy, disgustingly unclean." Like many words, the word *nasty* has less extreme meanings, but why use such a word when it could be misunderstood? Why does Pastor Greg avoid calling such talk "sinful"? It would have been more biblically correct for Pastor Greg to say, "no sinful talk." **However, the words "sin" and "sinful" are almost totally absent in *The Case*.** Pastor Greg does advise Bert to use the word *sin* when apologizing to his boss (p. 30) and Adams refers to this as sin in his discussion (p. 32). Pastor Greg does once refer to sin in a general way when he says, "Our sinful ways make us incompatible with God" (p. 63).

Aside from these instances, the words "sin" and "sinful" seem totally absent from the ten sessions in *The Case* in spite of the fact that there are numerous instances during the counseling where sin could be called *sin* but was not. In addition, Adams has an Appendix in which he lists "Some of the More Notable Ways in which Greg Brought This Case to a Successful End" (pp. 137-142). Out of the 100 items listed by Adams, only one mentions "sinners" (#99). If one looks up the word *sin* and all of its variations in the Bible, it is certainly a major biblical doctrine and needs to be identified as such when necessary. **Based upon Adams' ideal example, exemplified in *The Case*, nouthetic counseling seems to be an almost "sinless" approach.** This serious omission of the word *sin* is one possible result of problem-centered counseling. Problem-centered counselors become so problem-centered that they oftentimes overlook the biblical basics.

While Pastor Greg does not allow them to say these "nasty" things **to each other**, they are directed to say these same things to him **about each other**. This is a violation of Ephesians 5. Bert refers to Sue flying "into one of her tirades" (p. 11). Sue says of Bert, "He blew off steam at his boss yesterday, saying a few choice words, and the boss fired him. Disgusting, isn't it?" (p. 23). Some of the most petty things are said, such as Sue saying, "I think the second thing is his socks. He throws them on the floor at night, and I have to put them in the hamper the next morning" (p. 36).

Adams' list of 100 of "Some of the More Notable Ways in which Greg Brought This Case to a Successful End" reveals just how one-up (Pastor Greg) is and two-down (Bert and Sue) are and how problem-centered nouthetic counseling is. Unfortunately many will read the list as something to emulate and read it over and over again to obtain some gems for biblical counseling. Others will be intimidated, overwhelmed, and discouraged. Christ-centered ministry has no such complex and convoluted lists to follow, because no such lists are needed to minister.

The details and the drama of Bert and Sue are brought out in nouthetic counseling. If Bert truly loved his wife as Christ loved the church and gave Himself for her (Eph. 5:25) and if Sue were submissive to her husband and honored him (Eph. 5:24), they would not be sharing their marital problems with a third party. It is entirely unnecessary and unbiblical to share their marital problems with a third party. There is a better way, a biblical way that does not require this public airing of problems, but surely resolves them if they are resolvable. (See Part Three.)

31. Dishonoring Mother

Another problem that comes up has to do with Bert's mother. Sue begins with, "You see, Bert's mother lives two blocks away from us. So she's always coming over to our house. When she does, she is always trying to run our lives. She comes over and tells Bert what to think and do; and most of the time he listens to her…." Sue adds, "She's a Charismatic who is always getting a 'prophetic word' to reinforce what she tells us to do" (p. 92). Of course Bert's mother is not present to say whether or not she is trying to run their lives. Bert's mother's intent is assumed and believed. Here again they are encouraged to dishonor Bert's mother by speaking ill of her behind her back and placing her in the worst light.

Pastor Greg rightly refers to Genesis 2:24, "Therefore shall a man leave his father and his mother, and cleave unto his wife: and they shall be one flesh." He asks, "Why do you suppose there are no mother-in-law jokes about the woman's mother-in-law?" (p. 93). Regardless of the point he is trying to make, he is in error. We did an internet search for mother-in-law jokes and found such jokes about the husband's mother-in-law **and** about the wife's mother-in-law. So Greg's use of the word "no," meaning "not one," is false, which injects an added negative about Bert's mother, prior to suggesting that Bert go to his mother and:

> ... tell her in a kindly way that you are the head of a new family. Also tell her that, while happy to hear her suggestions, you will make your own decisions and not be persuaded to act as she wants simply because of who she is. And assure her that you will no longer allow any undue pressure or influence to interfere with your home life (p. 93).

Bert rightly asks, "Wouldn't that hurt her?" Pastor Greg says:

> She shouldn't be hurt if she handles what you say as a Christian should. We don't act on the basis of whether others take offense at what we do, but on the basis of whether or not it is what God wants us to do (pp. 93-94).

We agree with Pastor Greg that one should act "on the basis of whether or not it is what God wants us to do." However, we disagree with what he thinks God would want Bert to do. Is Greg attempting to change their circumstances by changing Bert's mother? We would also ask, why does Bert even have to tell his mother any of this since these are his decisions for his own behavior change. Then, if she asks why he is not doing things her way, he could gently explain his responsibilities to lead his family. We respect Bert's concern about the possibility of hurting his mother and would suggest that he pray about these needed changes and about how to accomplish his goal to be the head of the household in a way that would be pleasing to God and least hurtful to his mother.

At the next appointment, Bert tells Pastor Greg that he went to his mother and told her that, "while I would welcome advice, I would no longer allow anyone to meddle in our private affairs." Bert then says that his mother "told me off in non-Charismatic terms" (p. 102).

The commandment is clear: "Honour thy father and thy mother" (Exodus 20:12). There was no need for Bert to confront his mother as bluntly as he did and, all things considered, her response was predictable.

32. Non-Nouthetic Problems

There are several problems unrelated to nouthetic counseling that need to be noted, as they are serious distractions from *The Case* itself, **but are normal outcomes of problem-centered counseling.** There is a misrepresentation of Dr. James Dobson's position on divorce, the promotion of the Presbyterian Church versus the caricature of all Charismatics, and the implied denigration of the role of women in the church.

Dr. James Dobson

In reply to one of the questions on the PDI, Sue says:

> I didn't think that divorce was a possibility until a
> friend recently gave me a copy of an old article by
> Dr. James Dobson entitled, "Husband Who Feels
> Suffocated Needs To Be Set Free." He says that I can
> "open the cage door" and let my husband go free!!!
> Maybe that's the best thing to do. I've attached a
> copy of the article to this Inventory (p. 4).

This article by Dobson is repeatedly referred to throughout
The Case with Pastor Greg and Sue believing that Dobson is
recommending divorce (pp. 5, 49, 51, 54, 55, 63, 66). Pastor
Greg claims that Dobson advises "the opposite of what God
says in the Bible" (p. 55).

We obtained and read a copy of Dobson's article,
"Husband Who Feels Suffocated Needs To Be Set Free."[17] We
concluded that, contrary to what Pastor Greg and the couple
believed, the article does **not** advise divorce. To check this
out, we called Focus on the Family and were told that the
article does **not** advise divorce. We were told to visit a web
site to see Dobson's views on divorce.[18] We read Dobson's
views on divorce by reading his articles on "Relationships"
on that site. We conclude that Dobson's view is the same as
Adams' view, which is "that there are only two legitimate
reasons for believers to divorce, and then, there is no necessity
to do so" (p. 51).

As our readers know, we have authored a book and many
articles critical of Dobson.[19] However, here we must come to
Dobson's defense. His views on divorce have been misrep-
resented throughout *The Case*. Problem-centered counseling
often results in comments about what the counselee says,
such as about Dobson, that end up to be false, just as this one
is.

Presbyterians versus Charismatics

Adams refers at the beginning to the fact that Bert and Sue joined the "First Scriptural Presbyterian Church." Adams is Presbyterian and thus links *The Case* at the beginning to a Presbyterian church. Pastor Greg, the counselor in *The Case*, is obviously a Presbyterian pastor.

Bert's mother is a Charismatic, and, just as all Presbyterians are not the same, not all Charismatics are the same. Bert's mother, Mrs. Brown (her different last name is not explained), is a Charismatic who was earlier described as using a so-called "prophetic word" to support her advice to Bert and Sue (p. 92). During the special counseling session that included Bert's mother, she said to Pastor Greg, "Alright! I just received a word of knowledge telling me not to listen to anything you say…that you don't understand the Bible… that you are of the devil" (p. 110).

Pastor Greg refers to what he calls "the Charismatic problem" (p. 94). Adams' comments refer to the "Charismatic issue" (p. 95). Note that this is not just dealing specifically with Mrs. Brown, but with **all charismatics**. Pastor Greg recommends Adams' two books having to do with charismatics: *The Christian's Guide to Guidance* and *Signs and Wonders in the Last Days*.

Bert later says that he read the two books and then says, "I wish every Charismatic—including Mom—would read them!" (p. 122).

Pastor Greg responds, "Who knows? Perhaps the time will come when she will be willing—after she comes to recognizes [sic] the good 'Presbyterianism' has done for her and you" (p. 122). Later, Pastor Greg says of Bert's mother: "There's still a long way to go, but we're going to persist until we win her over completely—and I hope that even means to become a member of Scriptural Pres" [his church!] (p. 132).

While Pastor Greg cautions against "exaggeration" and "overstatement" (pp. 12, 92), it is obvious that he (therefore Adams) by characterizing **all** charismatics according to the fictional character of Bert's mother is guilty of both exaggeration and overstatement. Are there charismatics like Bert's mother? Yes. But there are other charismatics who would be in agreement with Adams criticisms of her, even though they would obviously disagree with his generalization describing all charismatics. The exalting of Presbyterians and the demeaning of charismatics through caricature and generalization are entirely uncalled for and distract from whether or not nouthetic counseling, per se, is biblical. Adams must be aware that his own Presbyterian denomination is accused of being legalistic, a generalization he would probably deny. We need to be careful about generalizing about other denominations. **Problem-centered counseling easily leads to such talk**.

Role of Women

Adams refers to "the flawed teaching in many women's Bible studies" (p. 66). Pastor Greg says, "Some women's study groups are an opportunity to meet and pool ignorance as they fill in white space in booklets that ask questions but provide no answers" (p.55). This, of course, is obviously true of some study groups of men, women, or couples. This is even true of some study groups led by pastors, elders, and other church leaders.

Sue later asks Pastor Greg, "Pastor, do you have a good women's Bible study group I can attend?" (p. 117). In response, Pastor Greg says, "So glad you asked. No, at the moment we don't. I know that there are one or two women who from time to time have expressed the same desire, but we've never had enough to form a group" (p. 117). He then encourages Sue to gather a group and says, "I'll get an elder to teach it. If I can't find one whose schedule is open, I'll teach it myself" (p. 118). Only "one or two women" in Pastor Greg's church "from time to time have expressed the same desire" for a "women's Bible study group"? How sad!

What comes across is that Pastor Greg is critical of "some women's study groups" and apparently does not encourage women in his church to become involved in one; but if they are interested either an elder or he himself will teach the class. Why not a woman to teach the class? This is more a reflection of Adams' particular Presbyterian orientation than a biblical mandate.

33. Bert and Sue in Christ-Centered Ministry

The Case is a clear example of a problem-centered biblical counseling system and typical counselor-counselee relationship. In Part Three we describe more fully "What Can Be Done." However, here we present a few ways of ministering to Bert and Sue in Christ-centered ministry. An overall difference is that we would emphasize the work of Christ in Bert and Sue **rather than focus on the specific problems they are experiencing.** (See Part Three.) Bert and Sue could be ministered to biblically without sinful communication and tale bearing that assume another's intent or heart attitude. **Problem-centered counseling, however, thrives on and even encourages such sinful communication.**

When people like Bert and Sue are experiencing such marital problems as they discuss, there is clearly something amiss in their walk with the Lord. Therefore we would emphasize how problems of living can actually be turned into opportunities for spiritual growth. (See Part Three.) We would want to help them see their situation from God's perspective. Their problems are a wake-up call to walk according to the Spirit rather than according to the flesh. Problem-centered nouthetic counselors may contend that working on behavior will result in walking according to the Spirit. Yet, we believe that people can make all kinds of external changes while continuing to walk according to the flesh and even strengthening it by doing so. After all, in problem-centered counseling the sinful flesh is given ample opportunity to express itself through gripes, complaints, and sinful conversations about one another and about people not present. Therefore, while ministering to Bert and Sue, rather than having to rely on such sinful, fleshly conversation in order to figure out what to counsel, we would be teaching and reminding them **that problems of living are opportunities for spiritual growth and change**.

It is clear from the description of Bert and Sue that they have no clue as to the real source of their problems, which is their own flesh and spiritual wickedness in high places (Eph. 6:12). They are each wanting the other person to change. They are struggling against each other instead of donning their spiritual armor, standing firm in faith, praying, and seeking God's will. As they grow spiritually, they will better know how to handle problems by grace through faith, prayer, worship, praise, thanksgiving, and obedience, and they will thereby be glorifying God and fulfilling His purposes. Yes, there are biblical admonitions for what they can do about certain specific problems, but they need to see the larger picture so that they will discover for themselves what they can do about their problems that would please God rather than self and Satan.

We would generally begin a time of ministry with prayer. Then we might ask Bert and Sue what help they are seeking from the Lord, because that would show us a general area in which He may be working in their lives. We would want to know enough to participate in what God is doing. When fellow believers, such as Bert and Sue, share problems, there is room for briefly hearing the general concern, as long as their description does not violate Scripture. However we would quickly redirect the conversation and attention away from their problems and onto Christ and all He has provided. We talk about ways to do this in Part Three. A concerted effort generally needs to be made to draw attention to Christ Himself, because people like Bert and Sue will almost always drift back into the direction of talking about their problems. If Bert and Sue are only looking for immediate solutions, they will miss the great opportunity to know Christ better and to grow spiritually.

Since Bert and Sue are presented as professing believers, we would encourage them to talk about their relationship with the Lord. Together Bert and Sue and the ministering couple could talk about the riches of what has been included in the death, burial, and resurrection of Christ and by our identification with Him. Some Christians have an incomplete understanding of redemption, why it was necessary and all it entails. We would want to make sure that Bert and Sue have a clear understanding and an ongoing gratitude for God's most precious gift. We would desire to help Bert and Sue see the utter sinfulness of the flesh, gaze at the perfections of Jesus Christ, and desire to reflect Him.

We may also ask Bert and Sue to talk about the blessings they have already received in Christ Jesus, such as God's immeasurable love, salvation, new life, imputed righteousness, freedom from the law of sin and death, eternal life, and "spiritual blessings in heavenly places in Christ Jesus" (Eph.

1:3). When attention is given to the magnificent love relationship that God has given every believer in Christ, there is a great opportunity for gratitude to flow and for the desire to do His will being kindled.

We would encourage Bert and Sue to look to Jesus in every trial, just as Jesus invites them in Matthew 11:28-30.

> Come unto me, all ye that labour and are heavy laden, and I will give you rest. Take my yoke upon you, and learn of me; for I am meek and lowly in heart: and ye shall find rest unto your souls. For my yoke is easy, and my burden is light.

How much better it is to help fellow believers grow in their walk with the Lord than to focus on the problem itself, for, as they yoke themselves with Christ in this problem and seek to follow Him through this trial, they will be prepared to face future difficulties. Moreover, they will learn to walk according to their new life in Christ, rather than according to the old ways of the flesh.

The conversation with Bert and Sue might include something like this: "In your circumstances there are some things you can do to grow spiritually, which may, in the long run, change the circumstances as well. What changes might Jesus plan to work in you through these circumstances?" If Bert and Sue talk about interpersonal problems or complain about each other or about other people, we would redirect the conversation away from how their spouse or others need to change to what Christ would want them to do and to how Christ can use their problems to bring about their spiritual growth.

However, more than working on specific issues, we would desire to help Bert and Sue "comprehend with all the saints what is the breadth, and length, and depth, and height; and to know the love of Christ, which passeth knowledge, that [they] might be filled with all the fullness of God" (Eph. 3:18-19), for it is out of this great love relationship that the new life flows. Thus, Bert and Sue should come to that place of praying something like this: "Lord, I want to know you better and love you more through this problem. Use me to accomplish your will in this situation." Indeed, Ephesians 3:20 applies to such a prayer for it says, "Now unto Him that is able to do exceeding abundantly above all that we ask or think, according to the power that worketh in us."

We would confront Bert and Sue with God's great love and redemptive power as we attempt to encourage their love for God so that there would be an outflowing of Christ's life. After all, the problem is not only that Bert is not loving his wife as Christ loves the church, but moreover that he is not living according to his new life in Christ, through which He would receive God's love and be able to love God enough to love his wife and to surmount problems even if circumstances do not change. As Bert and Sue's behavior is presented in *The Case*, it is clear that they had reverted to the flesh, and much of the effort they are making through counseling appears to be primarily works, motivated by the pastor's promise that their marriage will "sing." But, what if such a couple's marriage never sings? Will they still grow spiritually by grace through faith?

As Bert and Sue truly respond to God's love for them, they will love Him and desire to do His will. As they walk in this love relationship by grace through faith according to the new life He has given them, the Holy Spirit will enable them to love and obey Him more and more. Therefore all personal ministry should nurture that love for God. Bert and Sue will also show forth their love for God by loving one another and forgiving one another. We may also remind Bert and Sue that, because of His great love for them, God may even allow problems to build and fester to further conform them to the image of Christ. In love He will discipline them as they need it (Heb. 12). Therefore, they should not automatically expect things to be rosy right away, because they may need more tribulation to bring forth patience, experience, hope, and love (Romans 5:3-5).

When people like Bert and Sue are going through problems of living **they need to be encouraged to turn to God and worship Him daily.** (See Part Three.) People like Bert and Sue, who have been focused on their problems, definitely need a new perspective. They may need to be instructed about worship and about how they might worship God on a daily basis along with daily prayer and Bible reading. Bert and Sue need to learn or to remember that problems are calls to worship, for worship has to do with our recognition and submission to God's greatness, perfection, power, sovereignty, and authority over all of creation. They would be worshipping God when they place themselves under His authority and power and when they sanctify Him in their hearts (1 Peter 3:15) in meekness and holy fear. What better place is there to be when we are suffering?

As mentioned earlier, Part Three gives more details of "What Can Be Done" with Bert, Sue and others through Christ-centered ministry.

34. NANC

The following is **excerpted** from the NANC web site regarding "The Three Phases of NANC Certification":

Phase 1 – Training

1. Complete the Basic Training Course which covers the topic requirements by NANC. This training is to take place at a NANC approved training center.

2. You must complete a minimum of 10 hours of counseling observation of a NANC certified counselor....

3. A reading expectation of 1,000 pages from recommended reading list, 300 of which should be from theology text(s).

Phase 2 – Exams and Application
… Complete the NANC Theological and then the Counselor's exams....

Phase 3 – Supervision Counseling
…You are required to satisfactorily complete 50 hours of supervised counseling with a NANC Fellow during this phase. The 50 hours must be completed within one year of the date you passed your exams. At least 10 of these hours must be with the same counselee....

There are numerous biblically valid ministry approaches that do not require the formal intense and extended preparation required in nouthetic counseling.

In most cases both pastors and others are intimidated by all the hype in the biblical counseling movement. However the following is from a pastor who is not intimidated:

> I have just finished reading your latest publication, *Against "Biblical Counseling": For the Bible*. I just wanted to let you know how much I appreciate your willingness to go in print challenging the biblical counseling movement.
>
> I studied under Jay Adams at Westminster Seminary. I was greatly blessed under Adams and was convinced of the necessity to counsel from the Word of God as a pastor in a local church.

> I am blessed to pastor a church where I have preached the whole counsel of God. Very little counseling is needed apart from the preaching of the Word of God, and the counseling that is given each other by the members of this church.
>
> I have counseled couples and seen marriages saved. I have also seen rebellious children changed (some also hardened). The changes came not after weeks and years of "biblical counseling," but in the context of the fellowship of the church, and usually after one or two periods of confrontation or encouragement using the Word of God.
>
> After being barraged by all the solicitation about getting degreed or certified by conservative seminaries and the National Association of Nouthetic Counselors, I was beginning to feel inadequate again. Since reading your book, I will stay with the high calling of the biblical ministry in the local church.
>
> Thanks again for your work. I'm sure you will get much negative feedback. Just count me among those who are greatly appreciative of your book.

There are NANC members who charge for biblical counseling and also ones who are in separated-from-the-church biblical counseling centers. Adams says, "No one ought to hang out a shingle and set himself or herself up as a 'professional' biblical counselor."[20] In spite of Adams saying this, the National Association of Nouthetic Counselors (NANC) has had past and present board members who charge for biblical counseling. In other words, they are "professionals." In addition, NANC certifies many others who charge for biblical counseling. If NANC were truly biblical, no individual who charges would be allowed to be a member, especially a member of the board. For example, current NANC board member Dr. Ronald Allchin is the executive director of the Biblical Counseling Center in Arlington Heights, Illinois, which is a separated-from-the-church biblical counseling center and charges for biblical counseling. Allchin's web site gives the following information: "Initial Visit is 1½ hours long and the cost is $100. Follow-up Visits are 50 minutes long and the cost is $75.00."[21] In 2006 Allchin's Biblical Counseling Center listed a total revenue of $764,139.

35. CCEF
Idols-of-the-Heart Counseling

In Part One we briefly discussed the inner workings of the heart analysis (inner counseling approach) and described it as the opposite of behaviorism (outer counseling approach). We now reveal our concerns with the general teachings of that approach. Dr. David Powlison at the Christian Counseling and Educational Foundation (CCEF) provides a case study of Wally to exemplify this approach in an article titled "Idols of the Heart and 'Vanity Fair.'"[22] Powlison's article not only sets forth his expertise at "recycling" psychological counseling theories and therapies, but also reveals the fulfillment of his desire for CCEF to be "the ones who successfully will 'integrate' secular psychology," as stated years earlier in one of his articles in *The Journal of Pastoral Practice*:

> One of the ironies (whether it is bitter, humorous or sublime I am unsure!) attending the contemporary Christian counseling world is that **we, of all people, are the ones who successfully will "integrate" secular psychology.** "Integrationists" are too impressed with psychology's insights to be able to win them to

Christ. Integrationists have missed the point that the big question between Christians and secular psychologists is not, "What can we learn from them?" The big question is, "How can we speak into their world to evangelize them?" But it is also fair to say that presuppositionalists have missed that the big question between biblical counseling and Christian integrationists is not, "How can we reject and avoid them?" The big question is, "How can we speak constructively into their world?" The key to both big questions is an ability to **reframe everything that psychologists see and hold dear into biblical categories**. If we do our homework, then biblical counseling not only will be a message for the psychologized church. It will be a message for the psychologized world (bold added).[23]

Powlison saw problems with the way other people had been integrating psychology with the Bible. However, he fails to see that he is also too impressed with psychotherapeutic ideas, to the degree that he uses psychological teachings and techniques that encourage believers to sin against one another. His plan to "**reframe everything that psychologists see and hold dear into biblical categories**" has allowed him to simply organize and arrange those theories and techniques **that he believes to be useful** into a biblical framework. But, in doing so, the theories remain as deceptive as if they were in a secular framework. It is similar to the ways that people attempt to put evolutionism into a creationist framework. Either way, the Bible is compromised and people are deceived. Nevertheless, Powlison had dreams of winning those who didn't integrate biblically enough to his point of view:

At minimum there are thousands of Christians, psychologists, psychiatrists, social workers, college psychology majors, counselees drinking from a different well **who can be won by an approach that interacts with and radically reframes what enamors them about psychology** (bold added) .[24]

Here Powlison revealed his plan to appeal to other integrationists through reframing what "**enamors them about psychology**." But, what enamors people about psychology is its appeal to the flesh! Wouldn't Powlison thereby be appealing to a fleshly desire? In fact, should not love for and commitment to psychological theories and therapies be called an "idol of the heart"?

In his article "Idols of the Heart and 'Vanity Fair,'" Powlison reveals that he is continuing his quest to influence professional, psychologically trained Christians in the "helping professions." In the article he asks, "How do we legitimately and meaningfully connect the conceptual stock of the Bible and Christian tradition with the technical terminologies and **observational riches of the behavioral sciences**?" (p. 35, bold added). Throughout the article he shows how he connects idolatry, which he says is "the most frequently discussed problem in the Scriptures," to "the myriad significant factors that shape and **determine** human behavior," which are found in the psychological literature (p. 35, bold added).

Powlison argues that people develop idols of their hearts that usurp the love, devotion, trust, fear, service, attention, and delight that should go to God alone. Remembering that this is a metaphor, one could call anything an idol that usurps what belongs to God. However, in Scripture the references to idols generally have to do with actual idols, false gods, and false religions. In the New Testament the words translated *idol* refer to literal idols, false gods, or false religions.[25] Indeed, psychotherapy itself is a false religion. Dr. Thomas Szasz aptly describes psychotherapy when he says, "It is not merely a religion that pretends to be a science, it is actually a fake religion that seeks to destroy true religion."[26] Nevertheless, Powlison finds the idol motif useful for incorporating elements of this false religion of psychotherapy.

In his attempt to recycle secular psychology, Powlison takes verses from the Bible about the world, the flesh, and the devil and says: "It is striking how these verses portray a confluence of the 'sociological,' the 'psychological,' and the 'demonological' perspectives on idolatrous motivation" (p. 35). He then uses primarily the psychological and sociological theories to discuss inward motivation and outside influences. He later admits, "My analysis has been psycho-social" (p. 47).

While some of what he says in this section is biblically sound, he nevertheless relies on the psychological theories to fill out the particulars of his model of counseling. He says:

> That idolatries are both generated from within and insinuated from without has provocative implications for contemporary counseling questions. Of course, the Bible does not tackle our contemporary issues in psychological jargon or using our observational data. Yet, **for example, the Bible lacks the rich particulars of what psychologists today might describe as a "dysfunctional family or marital system"** only because it does not put those **particular pieces of human behavior** and mutual influence under the microscope. The "lack" is only in specific application (p. 36, bold added).

Powlison considers these to be important additions. He obviously regards some observational details and theoretical constructs, such as psychological "family systems," to be accurate, or why would he consider them important enough for filling in what the Bible appears to him to be lacking? However, we must always keep in mind that these details that are so important to Powlison have been **subjectively** observed, recorded, organized, and theorized by people with deceptive hearts who disagree with each other.

According to the *Concise Encyclopedia of Psychology*, "There are currently four major schools in family therapy: object relations theory, Bowen theory, structural family therapy, and communication theory."[27] Since these family systems are not alike and some of their underlying "particular pieces of human behavior" contradict one another, which ones would Powlison have a counselor use? One of them, Object Relations Theory, originated by Melanie Klein, tends to be very long term, is very Freudian, and concentrates on "unconscious denied projections."[28] The other three systems differ in their own ways from this approach and from each other. None of the family systems approaches has been shown to be superior to the others, and no one, including Powlison, has demonstrated that "particular pieces of human behavior" derived from family systems are of any use, except as fodder for his fanciful fossicking.

Powlison's retrofitting of both family systems and psychodynamic psychology into his system of idolatry opens the door to some very sinful ideas and practices. He says, "Idolatry is a problem both rooted deeply in the human heart and powerfully impinging on us from our social environment" (p. 38). He thus connects the metaphor "idols of the heart" with psychological and sociological influences that significantly influence behavior and that must therefore be mined from the depths of the heart through insight and analysis in a manner similar to insight psychology. Thus, to find, identify, and deal with these idols of the heart, the counselor must find out lots of details about the counselee's family relationships. Such will require extensive understanding about these things from psychology so that a person will know what kinds of relationships might influence the individual to form various kinds of so-called idols of the heart. In fact, Powlison's approach depends upon finding the psychological underpinnings of behavior and figuring out which idols of the heart he might decide they are. The idols-of-the-heart system appears to fit nicely with the use of the unconscious in psychotherapy, especially since there are so many possible hidden idols to look for, identify, and describe.

Powlison finds it necessary to explore lots of details of "particular pieces of human behavior" in the psychological literature regarding such things as the "classic alcoholic husband and the rescuing wife" who "are enslaved within an idol system whose components complement each other all too well" (p. 37). While he recognizes that psychology is inadequate regarding "the interface between responsible behavior, a shaping social milieu, and a heart which is both self-deceived and life-determining" (p. 38), he wrongly regards various teachings from psychology as helping biblical counselors understand the complexities of the inner person. He says:

> Humanistic psychologies see the interplay of inner desire/need with external fulfillment or frustration.... Ego psychologies see the twisted conflict between heart's desire and well-internalized social contingencies (p. 38).

Why do Christians even need to know that kind of information? If one follows Powlison's logic and use of psychology, one could conclude that the Christians of the past, prior to the rise of psychological counseling after

WWII, were handicapped because they did not have these latter day psychological "revelations."

Powlison says that "the behavioral sciences ... are idolatrously motivated" and "build into their charter and methodology a blindness to the essential nature of their subject" (p. 39). So, how can he trust what he calls the "rich particulars" (p. 36) from any of the psychological counseling literature? And, who decides which of the almost 500 conflicting approaches and which of the thousands of contradictory techniques have "rich particulars"?

Some years back we conducted a survey of the Christian Association for Psychological Studies (CAPS). CAPS members are psychologists of various kinds, many of whom practice psychotherapy and are committed to the integrationist view. We found in the CAPS survey how eclectic and, at the same time, different from one another these CAPS members were. Psychoanalytic, behavioristic, humanistic, and transpersonal psychologies were all possibilities for CAPS members. As a result of our survey of CAPS members, as well as information from numerous other psychologists, we state categorically that all of these psychologists (every one of them) would no doubt claim to use "sound psychological principles" and would say they are completely biblical or at least do not violate Scripture, even though they use a variety of the many available psychological approaches, many of which contradict one another.

Who is right and which one of these psychologized individuals should one believe and follow, including Powlison? As we describe and confront Powlison's recycled and reframed psychology, remember that all Christian psychologists are as completely certain, as he is, that they are truly biblical with their similar "recycling" and "reframing" psychology to "agree with the Bible." The difference is that Powlison appears to be arrogant enough to infer that he has it right; whereas all these other Christian psychologists have it wrong.

One is reminded of the Scripture of the blind leading the blind (Matt. 15:14). Even if Powlison picks and chooses according to the Bible itself, rather than imposing them into so-called biblical categories, his very picking may simply follow the idols of his own heart. There is really no end to guessing what idols of the heart may be hidden in one another's heart with so many possibilities and nuances that may come to mind, especially when one is well acquainted with the psychological wisdom of men.

Emphasizing the value of these psychological ideas detracts from his use of the Bible in his overall understanding. He says:

> Human motivation is … not strictly either psycho-dynamic or sociological or biological or any com-bination of these. These terms are at best metaphors for components in a unitary phenomenon which is essentially religious or covenantal. Motivation is always God-relational (p. 39).

Why doesn't he just stick with the final sentence from that quote, since the rest is unnecessary, superfluous, and down-right distracting? One wonders why he needs all of these psychological ideas to supplement Scripture since they cloud and distort the clear meaning of Scripture along the way.

Moreover, Powlison's system reduces all kinds of things to idols of the heart that must be searched out and decided upon. Not only must these idols be found, but their source also must be determined. While we can agree with Powlison regarding his statements that are biblically accurate, **we are opposed to problem-centered counseling conversations that come from seeking the source of the roots of behav-ior in ways similar to psychodynamic therapy as one can**

falsely biblicize them. In searching for the details to determine the specific idols in operation, much information must be unbiblically gleaned from a counselee, as will be seen in his case study of "Wally."

Problem-Centered Counseling with Idols for Every Problem

While Powlison and others at CCEF are in the business of searching for the idols of the heart, they are nevertheless problem-centered. His sixteen-page article begins with six-plus pages teaching about the idols of the heart and presenting the theoretical construct of his unbiblical problem-centered recycling approach to counseling as conducted by the CCEF idols-of-the-heart counselors. Next, the case of Wally reveals that the counselor works to unveil the heart and unravel the layers so that he can see what idols might be there, determine how they got there, decide how they function, and then transform the hidden motivations of the counselee into idols of the heart. The entire analysis is problem-centered and psychologically dependent. Although no dialogue is presented, it is clear that Powlison had to spend lots of time conversing about Wally's problems in order to speculate about what's going on inside and how to fix the problems from the inside out. **In other words, the counselor, whose own heart is "deceitful and desperately wicked," must see into another person's "deceitful and desperately wicked heart" to deal with the problems of living, in spite of the Lord Himself declaring that He is the One who searches the heart (Jeremiah 17:9).**

Powlison seems to turn almost everything into idolatry. He says: "Idolatry becomes a concept with which to comprehend the intricacies of both individual motivation and social conditioning. The idols of the heart lead us to defect from

God in many ways" (p. 37). Turning almost everything into idolatry is a convenient way for him to imbed the psychological counseling concepts he likes into his form of "biblical counseling." He justifies this by saying that "behavioral sins are always portrayed in the Bible as 'motivated' or 'ruled' by a 'god' or 'gods.'" However, he fails to support this "always" statement with Scripture. There are many instances in the Bible in which it was simply lust or sinful desire that motivated sinful actions. For instance, what god or gods motivated David to commit adultery with Bathsheba? There is no hint in Scripture that this was a god, unless, of course, David was his own god, but then one could understand every sinful motivation as due to idolatry of the self. And, if one does that, then one does not have to develop or learn an entire pantheon of idols, as in Powlison's idols-of-the-heart system. It really all boils down to God's way or my way, but if we do that, we have no justification for bringing in the psychological wisdom of men

What the Bible Says about Idols of the Heart

The word *heart* often signifies the inner man in Scripture and the word *idols* may be used metaphorically even though idols appear to be literal throughout Scripture. **However, there is no biblical basis for searching for idols of the heart as done by Powlison.** The phrase "idols of the heart" is absent from the major translations of the Bible. However, Powlison refers to Ezekiel 14:1-8 in his attempt to support his use of "idols of the heart." Ezekiel was a prophet of God and therefore received direct revelation from God: "Son of man, these men have set up their idols in their heart" (v. 3). When the men set up idols **IN** their heart, the idols were placed in the center of their devotion. There is a great difference between the two prepositions *IN* and *OF*. The word *OF* indicates belonging to, proceeding from, being a component, connection, or possession. Thus, the expression "idols **OF** the heart" indicates belonging to the heart, being an aspect of the heart itself, proceeding forth from the heart. The men setting up "idols IN their heart" in Ezekiel means that they have put them there, figuratively speaking, because of their heartfelt devotion to literal idols.

Ezekiel was not analyzing the men psychologically to gain insight into their heart to determine why they were doing what they were doing. Therefore Powlison's use of Ezekiel 14 to support his psychologically analytical scheme removes the context and distorts the meaning. In the context of Ezekiel 14:1-8, a comparison is being made between the men's outward worship of Jehovah and their real love and worship of the idols. The contrast is between their outward, insincere worship and inner, true devotion. Regarding Ezekiel 14:3, Matthew Poole (1624-1679) described these men as "resolved idolaters, their hearts were totally addicted to their idolatrous worship and ceremonies."[29] Because of the rampant idolatry at the time, those "idols in their heart" would have been related to actual idols, false religions, and false gods of the surrounding nations for which they had a heartfelt devotion.

To support his use of "idols of the heart," Powlison claims that 1 John 5:21, "Little children, keep yourselves from idols," must refer metaphorically to "idols of the heart" if the Scripture is to apply over time. However, the apostle John did not expand the meaning of idols and every reader at the time would have known he was referring to literal idols and false religions, because that was what many of them had left behind and could yet be tempted to worship. Turning these idols into metaphors to keep the Bible relevant to all periods of time is totally unnecessary since images, icons, statues, stones, and other physical forms of idols continue to this day and will continue until the return of Christ. Nevertheless, as mentioned earlier, the word *idols* can be used in a metaphorical sense. However, the Bible does not teach that there are idols in the heart that must be searched out by another human being through a psychologically contaminated system of insight and analysis. The Bible provides precise words regarding the source of sinful attitudes, thoughts, and motives, such as the word *flesh* used metaphorically throughout the New Testament in contrast to the word *Spirit*. Moreover, God has given every believer the Holy Spirit and the Word to enable each one to choose to follow the flesh or the Spirit.

Even if one is to use *idols of the heart* metaphorically, the Bible does not direct believers to search out one another's heart. Instead, the Lord does this. However, this latter-day psychological wisdom of men has given Powlison and his colleagues the notion that, by analyzing a counselee through extensive, expensive conversations focused on the counselee and his problems, they can know the idols of the counselee's heart.

Even the idea of believers searching for idols of their own hearts is absent from Scripture. The Holy Spirit is the indwelling counselor and is faithful to convict believers of their sinful actions, attitudes, and motivations. While believers are to examine themselves, the examination has to do with whether they are walking according to the Spirit by grace through faith. For instance, 2 Corinthians says, "Examine yourselves, whether ye be in the faith; prove your own selves. Know ye not your own selves, how that Jesus Christ is in you, except ye be reprobates?" The point of the verse has to do with the new life in them. Are they living by the new life Christ purchased for them or by their old fleshly ways? This kind of examination places more attention on the person of Christ than on the self. It's a reminder for believers to remember who they are in Christ. When they turn to Him they are enabled to walk according to the Spirit rather than the flesh. Hunting for idols, figuring out how they interact with other people's idols, and trying to get rid of them gives too much attention to the self, just like secular psychology. **The focus in psychology is the self; the focus in Christianity is Jesus Christ. Believers are to be "looking unto Jesus, the author and finisher of our faith" (Hebrews 12:2).** In fact, it is by looking unto Jesus that believers are transformed into His image: "But we all, with open face beholding as in a glass the glory of the Lord, are changed into the same image from glory to glory, even as by the Spirit of the Lord" (2 Cor. 3:18).

36. "Case Study and Analysis"

The actual dialogue and methodology of questioning, responding, and teaching are absent from Powlison's article. It is simply an analysis of poor Wally according to the so-called idols of his heart, how they developed, how he is "abused" by them (p. 42), and how they interact with the idols of the people in his environment. Powlison begins his case study and analysis by saying that he is "using a case study of a hurt-angry-fearful person" named Wally (p. 41). Powlison admits, "The external details of this case study are fabricated" (p. 41). We must add that, if they are fabricated, so are Wally's idols (inner details), as well as the account of how this kind of counseling helped Wally (p. 43). Nonetheless, **the case study does reveal how problem-centered and psychologically self-centered the idols-of-the-heart counseling is.**

Powlison begins by describing Wally:

> Wally is a 33-year-old man. He has been married to
> Ellen for eight years. They have two children. He is a

highly committed Christian. He works for his church half time as an administrator and building overseer and half time in a diaconal ministry of mercy among inner city poor. He and his wife sought counseling after an explosion in their often-simmering marriage. He became enraged and beat her up. Then he ran away, threatening never to come back. He reappeared three days later, full of guilt, remorse, and a global sense of failure (p. 41).

Powlison describes Wally's "longstanding problems" as "anger, inability to deeply reconcile, threats of violence alternating with threats of suicide, depression, workaholism alternating with escapism, a pattern of moderate drinking when under stress, generally poor communication, use of pornography, and loneliness" (p. 41).

Violations of Scripture

Problem-centered counseling by its very nature is loaded with sinful communication and thereby often violates the very Word of God that biblical counselors claim to follow. In Part One we gave five of many violations of Scripture that occur in problem-centered counseling. We enumerate them briefly in the following and identify the biblical violation.

The following is said of Wally's father:

Wally's father was a critical man, impossible to please. "If I got all A's with one B, it was 'What's this?' If I mowed and raked the lawn, it was 'You missed a spot behind the garage'" (p. 41).

Throughout the counseling it is very clear that Wally dishonors his parents and is encouraged to do so. Otherwise there would not be so many negative statements about his father. However, such sinful talk is part of the process of problem-centered counseling and especially when the counselor is looking for psychological determinants of behavior in the unconscious. Powlison denies that he is doing that; however he is very close to it. He says:

> These forces and shaping influences neither determine nor excuse our sins. **But they do nurture, channel, and exacerbate our sinfulness in particular directions.** They are often atmospheric, invisible, **unconscious influences** (p. 44, bold added).

Wally describes his mother as "well-meaning, nice, but ineffective, totally intimidated by my Dad" (p. 41). Here he is dishonoring his mother. There appears to be no concern about such sinful talk during this kind of counseling. In fact, problem-centered, idols-of-the-heart counseling depends on this kind of information or misinformation. After all, this is only from Wally's perspective. One really hears nothing positive about his poor mother throughout the entire case study. Did she feed and clothe him as he was growing up? Did she take care of him when he was sick? Did Wally have one ounce of gratitude for his parents? No need to mention those kinds of things in problem-centered counseling. After all, the counselor is seeking out problems, with the counselee fixated on himself and his problems.

Wally describes his wife, Ellen, this way: "bossiness, nagging, controlling me, not supporting me or listening to me" (p. 41). Whether Ellen had anything to say in the matter is not clear, since this appears to be individual counseling with Wally, even though thy both sought counseling. Powlison describes these people as if he knows them personally, when he really only knows Wally's parents through what Wally says, which is second-hand and obviously biased. Is that the way to know anybody? Moreover, he draws all kinds of conclusions about them and how they have influenced Wally with only Wally's say-so in an environment that leads to bad-mouthing the very people Wally is to respect and love. Much is said about Wally's father, mother, and wife and also about Wally himself. We are less concerned about what Wally says about himself, but very concerned about his sinful descriptions of his parents and his wife.

As in most problem-centered counseling case studies, Powlison utilizes the problems in Wally's life to demonstrate his model and methodology and to convince the reader of the effectiveness of this kind of counseling. However, Powlison's insights are built upon a structure of biblical violations in what Wally communicates and, very importantly, on the fact that it is doubtful, as in most counseling, that Wally's descriptions are entirely accurate and trustworthy. As one becomes experienced in counseling, one learns that if the parents and the wives of the Wallys in counseling were asked to comment about how they are described, a different picture would emerge, invalidating both what the Wallys have said and what the problem-centered counselors have concluded through inferences, intuitions, and insights along with speculations and guesses. Besides the serious violations of Scripture, one of the biggest drawbacks of problem-centered counseling is the untrustworthiness of what is said and heard and, thereby, what is unsaid and unheard. For instance, throughout an entire year of counseling, the counselor may never even guess that the counselee has been sexually unfaithful during this entire time unbeknownst to the counselor and the spouse. Lots of talking with much analytical discussion and speculation often passes over the real problem.

Because of the untrustworthiness of what counselees say, Wally's descriptions of his "critical" father and "ineffective" mother should be regarded as gossip (Proverbs 18:8). Wally's accusations of his wife "nagging and controlling" are a violation of Ephesians 5. Wally's description of the past week with an element of blame (p. 41) is unbiblical (Phil. 3:13-14). Wally presents himself as a victim and Powlison agrees (p. 42). And, most obvious, as we said earlier, Wally has dishonored his father and mother (Exodus 20:12 and Eph. 6:1-2).

Powlison does not divert Wally from his sinful tale-bearing, discrediting of his wife, blaming the past, playing the victim, and dishonoring his parents. Instead, Powlison participates in these sins and even amplifies them. He says:

> We see the dominion of a father whose leadership style was that of a tyrant-king, not that of a servant-king promoting the well-being of his son. In essence, he lied, bullied, enslaved, and condemned (p. 42).

Notice how Powlison, like the par excellence problem-centered counselor he is, believes Wally and says, "Wally's father was a critical man, impossible to please" (p. 41). Powlison represents Wally's father as saying, "You must please *me* in whatever way I determine" (italics in original, p. 42). Powlison later refers to "Wally's demanding and unpleasable father" (p. 45). Considering that no one can hear from Wally's deceased father, these are extreme accusations. They demonstrate Powlison's penchant for believing and transmitting gossip and his creative writing abilities more than the truth. All of this is part and parcel of problem-centered psychodynamic therapy.

Powlison buys into the psychological victimhood idea. **He describes Wally as a victim of his parents, of his wife, of the circumstances of his childhood, and even of his idols.** Powlison says:

> Wally was conditioned to be very concerned with what significant people thought of him. At the same

time Wally bought the idol. He is simultaneously a **victim** and guilty. He was abused by powerful idols operative within his family system. He also instinctively both bought into those idols and produced his own competitive idols (p. 42, bold added).

Powlison also says, "Wally is psychologically controlled by a lush variety of false gods" (p. 44). Once counselors start down the "psychological side" and the "sociological side," as Powlison does, these sides become primrose paths on which one can trot out every possible creatively concocted interpretation limited only by one's imagination.

Helping Wally see himself as needy, emotionally wounded, and having been harmed, negatively influenced, or disappointed by others softens the biblical reality of responsibility, sin, and guilt, where the only true remedy is the cross of Christ and ongoing dependence on Christ for inner change and spiritual growth. Softening responsibility, sin, and guilt with all kinds of explanations of what happened in the formation of the inner person and how the inner person currently functions provides a different remedy (explaining and fixing the flesh) and ongoing dependence on the counselor, at least until Wally can identify and control the idols that Powlison points out. All in all, much of this sounds like a very fleshly pursuit. In fact, this kind of counseling would work just as well with professing Christians who are not truly born again.

The more Wally sees himself as a victim, the further he will move away from a recognition of his own depravity, the necessity of the cross, and love for the Lord for His saving grace and for the new life He has given. The more he sees himself as a victim, the less gratitude he will have for his parents, his wife, and the Lord Jesus Christ. While there are true victims, focusing on their victimhood does not strengthen them anywhere but in the flesh.

In his book titled *A Nation of Victims: The Decay of the American Character*, Charles Sykes says:

> The triumph of the therapeutic mentality ... insisted upon seeing the immemorial questions of human life as problems that required solutions. The therapeutic culture provided both in abundance: The therapists transformed age-old human dilemmas into psychological problems and claimed that **they (and they alone) had the treatment** (bold added).[30]

Similarly Powlison sees the complexities of the inner life as problems that require solutions. Here we have a psychospiritual therapeutic mentality where the idols-of-the-heart counselors are the experts and where "**they (and they alone) [have] the treatment**."

Powlison begins his section on "Multiple Idols" by saying, "We become infested with idols," almost as if they are external things like germs or pests (p. 43). If we are infested, is it really all our fault or is it that we really should not have left the honey on the counter to attract the ants or is it that we have neglected to call the exterminator? We know from Scripture that sin indwells all humans and that the "old man" is described as "corrupt according to the deceitful lusts" (Eph. 4:22). These are inordinate desires that indwell the inner person. Jesus did not die to save us from the influences in our lives or from some sort of infestation from without; He came to save us from our sinful condition and sins committed. Furthermore, He gave believers new life, not an idols-of-the-heart extermination manual.

One Up / One Down

Powlison's statement, "We become infested with idols" has the pronoun "we." That is important because Powlison's possible "one-up" idols have a difficult time dealing with Wally's idolatrous mixture of desire for approval and resistance to being in the "one-down" position." Powlison says:

> The idolatrous patterns in Wally's relationship with his father manifest in other relationships. Wally has had ongoing problems with authority figures in school, the military, work, and the church.... Naturally, he brings this same pattern into the counseling relationship, with all the challenges that creates for building trust and a working relationship. He continues to manifest a typical stew of associated problems: a slavish desire to be approved, a deep suspicion that he won't be approved, a stubborn independency (p. 43).

Poor Wally! Even without being supposedly "infested with idols," the one-up/one-down counseling relationship alone can create that kind of mix, especially for men. Nevertheless, the counselor, being in the one-up position and having to engender trust, must exert his superiority, and this he will be able to do if he has a system with shibboleths known primarily to him. Because of the kind of counseling he does, Powlison cannot afford to meet on an equal basis at the foot of the cross in mutual care. After all, CCEF does charge money for counseling.

Besides believing that he can discern idols of the heart in other people, Powlison makes the following claim: "Biblical counsel, **the mind of Christ about Wally's life**, can be given" (p. 43, bold added). The structure of that last sentence has "the mind of Christ about Wally's life" in the position of an appositive after the words "biblical counsel."

An appositive is a grammatical form that gives an alternative meaning or further meaning to the noun preceding it. Thus in essence and in the context it is given, Powlison is claiming that, through his idols-of-the-heart system, biblical counsel can be given that is, in essence, "the mind of Christ about Wally's life." In fact, he says:

> As we have indicated, Wally's mass of behaviors, attitudes, cognitions, value judgments, emotions, influences, *et al.* can be understood right down to the details utilizing the biblical notion of idolatry (p. 46).

What a claim! Actually what Powlison has really done is simply categorize all these things and renamed them as idols. In other words, he understands where everything fits into his preconceived grid. And this is "the mind of Christ about Wally's life"?

The power structure is very clear with the counselor in the one-up position giving Wally in the one-down position "the mind of Christ" about his life. While Scripture tells believers that they have the mind of Christ (2 Cor. 2:16), it does **not** say we have the mind of Christ for someone else. The entire structure of the counseling is one-up/one-down with the counselor analyzing Wally and describing him in a very demeaning manner. Here are a few examples of how Powlison describes Wally:

> He oscillates between "flame-thrower and the deep freeze." On the one hand he can be abrasive, manipulative, angry, and unforgiving. On the other hand he withdraws, feels hurt, anxious, guilty, and afraid of people (p. 41).

> Wally continues to play out a three-fold theme. First, he typically rebels against certain dominant "suc-

cessful people" cultures. Second, he finds his validity in the affirmation of a "down-and-out" subculture. Third, all the while he acts in idiosyncratic pride to create his own culture-of-one in which he plays king, and his opinions on anything from the dinner to eschatology are self-evident truth (p. 43).

Certain gentle-faced idols—the mass media, professional sports, and the alcohol industry—woo him with temporary compensations and false, escapist saviors from the pressures generated by his slavery to the harsh, terrifying idols which enslave and whip him along at other times: "I must perform. I must prove myself" (p. 43).

Anyone who reads this article who intends to be counseled with this form of counseling should be prepared to be viewed, analyzed, and described psychologically in similarly demeaning ways. Just as we wonder how Wally's parents and wife would respond to his descriptions of them, we wonder how Wally would respond to such demeaning descriptions of himself in this "expert/dummy" relationship where the one who does the naming is the one who has the position of power, from which he claims to see into and analyze Wally's heart.

Methodology

Nowhere in the article does Powlison explain how he enables Wally to get rid of his vast infestation of idols or how to control them when they come into contact with other people's idols. Evidently the methodology is centered on the analysis of Wally according to the idols of the heart and then relating this so-called wisdom to Wally. Powlison says:

"Wisdom, the nourishing and honeyed tongue, can make satisfying and convicting sense of things, and Wally can learn to live, think, and act with such wisdom" (p. 43). In other words after much conversation Powlison can, with his "honeyed tongue," sweetly point out Wally's many sins in terms of idols so that Wally can do the work of improving himself. That is exactly what most psychological counseling ends up being—self help according to whatever theoretical structure has been conveyed through the many expensive hours of counseling.

Therefore all that is necessary is to analyze Wally according to the idols of the heart, reveal those idols to Wally, teach Wally about how they motivate him, and possibly suggest tactics to disarm them—not that they are actually there, but that Powlison has said so. With this knowledge Wally may actually feel better about himself, in that he was not fully responsible for the formation of these powerful "idols" (p. 42ff). Maybe the idea is that if Wally can feel better about himself, he'll be willing to work on these idols that Powlison names. He may also feel empowered because he knows the names of the idols and understands how Powlison thinks they operate in his life. He may also be willing to follow along because now he's learning how to gain personal power himself by becoming a namer of idols, much like people gain a false sense of power in naming the temperament types of other people. After all there is power in being the one who names or at least in knowing the names. Wally may thereby become more self-confident with this information and even be able to control those "idols" to some degree by the power of the flesh, which doesn't mind as long as it is in control.

Powlison claims to know enough about what goes on in Wally's "complex heart and complex world to minister helpfully to him" (p. 43). Powlison does not even have to know all these things about Wally, let alone analyze them and talk-talk-talk about them. God gave the method of communication: preach the Gospel and teach about sanctification. This is what was done in the early days of the church where people truly knew that they were new creatures in Christ.

The Bible does not give any indication that believers need to know anyone's "complex heart and complex world to minister helpfully to him." **In fact, a believer does not even need to know the sins, sinful motivations, or what Powlison identifies as the idols of the heart of another believer in order to effectively minister the life of Christ and encourage sanctification.** If believers need to know a fellow believer's "complex heart and complex world to minister helpfully to him," there would be clear instruction about this in the New Testament. Powlison's fascination and confidence in the psychological wisdom of men have corrupted his model. In actuality all he has is external manifestations of the inner person from which he must assume, surmise, guess, and fabricate according to the system he has contributed to developing. That's really all the Puritan pastors had as they sought to search out the idols of the heart in their parishioners. In their attempt to help people, they also diverted away from full dependence on Scripture here, and, in doing so, prepared Christians to become more interested in finding out about the inner man. A book with the subtitle *From Salvation to Self-Realization* traces this history and reveals that the Puritan investigation into the inner man with the metaphor "idols of the heart" set the stage for the current-day acceptance and eagerness for counseling psychology.[31]

The "idols-of-the-heart" methodology cannot really bring accurate knowledge regarding the condition of the heart. It is limited to external indications of what might fit into their preconceived pantheon of idols. After observing

Wally's actions and listening to what he says about himself, the idols-of-the-heart counselor fits his own subjective observations into his idolatrous system. It's really all guesswork. Powlison claims Wally does not know what is going on inside his own heart, and, if truth be known, neither does Powlison. However, with a system that groups certain actions, words, responses, and emotional expressions under various categories of idols, one could easily do that for oneself and others—and be completely wrong.

Yes, there will be some connection in some of the more obvious ones, especially those tendencies that most people have, such as one of their favorites, which is "fear of man." Such feelings are common to mankind. Because many of the idols they have named have to do with various feelings and sinful attitudes and actions, counselees will very possibly admit to various idols that represent even fleeting feelings and temptations. In fact, some counselees will be more vulnerable than others to becoming overwhelmed with a whole host of idols assigned to them during counseling. Indeed, this reminds us of the title of Dr. Tana Dineen's book *Manufacturing Victims: What the Psychology Industry is Doing to People*.[32] A parallel might be something like Manufacturing Idols: What the Idols-of-the-Heart Counseling Industry is Doing to Christians.

After Wally learns all about his idols and the idols of those in his environment, he will still have quite a time keeping track of all of them and remembering which idol is interacting with which idols of the people around him. How can he even give attention to the Lord Jesus when he has to be watching out for all the supposed idols of his heart and those of people in his environment? It sounds like an arduous self-centered requirement. Moreover, he might easily be blindsided by some so-called idols of which he is yet unaware. Then what? How much easier to follow the Bible and live by the new life Christ has given where Christ gets all the credit and glory rather than the person who is busy dealing with everyone else's idols in addition to his own. More will be said about this shortly in "Wally and Christ-Centered Ministry."

This type of counseling is a very deceptive practice because people are led to believe that some people (i.e., "experts") can see right through them. Worse than that, they will think they now know their inner idols and motivations and be further deceived. Then, if they don't feel or do better after all the counseling, they will assume that there must be more idols lurking in the wings and run back to the counselor who can supposedly see inside them. They may become thoroughly dependent on the expensive counselor to name the idols supposedly hidden in the heart, which in this kind of counseling seems to resemble a Freudian-type of powerful unconscious that drives behavior.

37. An Idolatrous System

Idols-of-the-heart biblical counseling is truly an idolatrous system. Just as the Israelites copied the nations around them and adopted their idols, so also have those who developed and use the idols-of-the-heart system been attracted to the psychological counseling systems of the world around them and then adopted aspects of those systems. As Powlison correctly says:

> With good reason both Old and New Testaments abound with warnings against participating in pagan cultures and associating with idolaters, fools, false teachers, angry people, and the like. Our enemies not only hurt us, they also tempt us to be like them. False voices are not figments which the individual soul hallucinates. "World" compliments "flesh" to

constitute monolithic evil: the manufacture of idols instead of worship of the true God (p. 44).

Yet, that is exactly what recycling is. It is "participating in pagan cultures." Even Christians who have a strong grasp of Scripture seem to be easily tempted and drawn into the scientific-sounding academia of psychological theories and therapies. Indeed the world of psychological counseling compliments the flesh "to constitute monolithic evil: the manufacture of idols instead of worship of the true God." Here the hierarchy of idols includes such individuals as Sigmund Freud, Carl Jung, Alfred Adler, Abraham Maslow, Carl Rogers, and many others, primarily from the psychoanalytic and humanistic branches of psychotherapy. Even though Powlison is really talking about idols of the heart, he actually gives a good description of the idols of psychology when he says:

> Such false gods create false laws, false definitions of success and failure, of value and stigma. Idols promise blessing and warn of curses for those who succeed or fail against the law (p. 42).

That is really an excellent evaluation of the fountains from which Powlison recycles and reframes to form his problem-centered idols-of-the-heart system. Indeed, he must have some love for those systems. Else why would he think it necessary to imbibe, recycle, and reframe from those various idolatrous systems and seek to fit them into "biblical categories"?

This polluted cistern of problem-centered, psychological counseling from which Powlison and other problem-centered integrationists have been drawing is loaded with the rottenness of evil speaking. Those who engage in problem-centered counseling, no matter what their positive motives may be, are often engendering strife in families as people talk behind one another's backs and say all manner of evil about them, whether true or false. When people speak evil of others, they actually increase their negative feelings towards them to justify having said bad things. When people focus on how bad things are, they fail to see what is good. Rather than nurturing gratitude, these counselors may be nourishing ingratitude towards God and others. Rather than nurturing love for God and others, they may be feeding self-love and pride. Evil speaking of others is not edifying to believers (Eph. 4:29, 31). Therefore counseling that depends on it is sinful and will fail to nurture spiritual growth.

Powlison's various justifications for using psychology fit well with his idols-**of**-the-heart motif. In fact that very motif almost makes those additions sound acceptable since the Bible does speak of men with "idols **in** their heart" (Ezekiel 14:3) and also because the Puritan divines were fascinated with the idea. But, the more biblical an unbiblical system sounds, the more deceptive it is, compared with the more obvious "psychologizing and moralizing" of which he accuses other "Christians who seek to help their fellows" (p. 48).

Regarding the weaknesses of typologies and the DSM categories, Powlison says, "In fact, they are not explanations for anything but are simply ways of describing clusters of symptoms" (p. 45). The same can be said about his idols-of-the-heart system. Regarding the typologies, he says,

> Typologies are pseudo-explanations. They are descriptive, not analytical, though as conceptual tools for various psychologies and psychotherapies they pretend to explanatory power.... Current typologies are not helpful for exposing the real issues in the lives of real people.... At worst, they are bearers

of misleading conceptual freight, for they duck the idolatry issues.(p. 45).

Almost the same could be said for Powlison's system, except for the final phrase about "duck[ing] the idolatry issues."

Powlison's intent seems to be true spiritual growth on the part of the believer. He appears to want to disable that flesh when he says, "The rampant and proliferating desires (plural) of the flesh contend with the Spirit and clamor for our faith and obedience." He sees that psychological systems fail at this. Nevertheless, he has borrowed numerous bits and pieces from those very systems and fails to see that he has brought in too much of the world to truly enable people to have victory over the flesh. One does not overcome the flesh with fleshly contaminated weapons. It is the Spirit that wars against the flesh as the believer exercises faith in the finished work of Christ. At one point, Powlison even says:

> Awareness of spiritual warfare also helps shake us out of the behavioral science mindset which tempts us to think about people psycho-socially rather than with respect to God" (p. 46).

After such a statement we wonder why he remains committed to using psychology. Evidently in his case the shaking was temporary. He probably should have ended that sentence with: "rather than **both** psycho-socially **and** with respect to God." After all he uses both.

Powlison has turned his psychologically tainted system into a necessity for all Christians who would minister to fellow believers, for he says: "If we would help people have eyes and ears for God, we must know well which alternative gods clamor for their attention" (p. 44). However, the old self is the primary false god for everyone and that is why the flesh must be put off and denied. Self is the very essence of the psychological systems that have a host of things to look for in the self and a myriad of systems that must be learned and followed. If a believer were to have "eyes and ears for God," which seems like a rather pompous description for anyone these days, they would certainly not need Powlison's system of idols, no matter how those idols seem to fit the various manifestations of the flesh. If one is to have "eyes and ears for God" one must be much in His Word and in His presence. One does not have to memorize the names of an ever-expanding hierarchy of idols.

Turning "inordinate, life-ruling desires," and "human lust, craving, yearning, and greed demand" into idols removes them one step away from the person himself. An idol is not simply a sinful tendency of the flesh; it is still external to the person. It's not Wally; it's his idols that are the problem. They may be manifestations of his flesh, but they are not the totality of his flesh, which must be denied and put off. Wally's primary problem is that he is living according to what the Bible calls the "old man" rather than by the new life Christ purchased for every believer. This focus on idols does not disable or disarm the flesh, even though one may learn to rearrange the power structure of the so-called idols. In doing so, Wally might succeed in overcoming some of his anger, rebellion, fear, and sexual lust by strengthening his self-confidence and pride, even while believing he is becoming a truly humble servant.

Powlison says, "It is a curious but not uncommon phenomenon that a biblically literate person like Wally has no effective grasp on the idols of his own heart and the temptations of the particular Vanity Fair which surrounds him" (p. 47). Even a biblically literate person would have to learn the idols-of-the-heart system because they are not named as idols in the Bible. In this kind of counseling, one has to learn the system. Wally must have been aware of his own sins and sinfulness and of the sins of those around him. Otherwise he could not have communicated them to Powlison. Wally just had never thought of turning them all into idols that he could manipulate and manage. But now he has a way to look at his own life without becoming overwhelmed with the utter sinfulness of his flesh and without having to own up to the fact that he is evidently trying to live the Christian life through the power of the flesh.

We also wonder how biblically literate Wally is regarding the teachings about the new life in Christ and what sanctification is really all about. He seems to have been involved in a great deal of self effort that did not succeed, and now he has embarked on a new path of self-effort where he has to keep track of all his idols and the idols of those around him. Wally needs to get back into the Bible itself and find his freedom in Christ.

Powlison says he has focused on "the issue of diagnosis" because "biblical diagnosis bridges immediately into biblical treatment" (p. 48). However, his analysis and treatment are not truly biblical. They are an amalgamation of psychological theories and therapies and the Bible, all wrapped together with four words, "idols of the heart," eisegeted to fit his commitment to recycling (integration). Believers do not need such a complex, convoluted psychologically contaminated system to discern whether they are walking according to the flesh or the Spirit.

The Flesh or the Spirit?

Powlison appears to consider this idols-of-the-heart counseling to be a means of sanctification. He speaks of salvation and then says, "But the ongoing work of renewal must engage him [Wally] genuinely over the particular patterns of idolatry that functionally substitute for faith in Christ" (p. 44). But, does an analysis of the flesh really enable a person to walk according to the Spirit? Prior to the current psychological era and prior to Powlison's idols-of-the-heart counseling there was a simple, understandable message: The Gospel, including the good news of Christ indwelling the believer through the Holy Spirit. God has given the means of sanctification. No help was needed from the psychological wisdom of men. Paul speaks of salvation and the sanctification process following salvation in Colossians as a mystery that has been revealed to believers:

> Even the mystery which hath been hid from ages and from generations, but now is made manifest to his saints: To whom God would make known what is the riches of the glory of this mystery among the Gentiles; which is Christ in you, the hope of glory: Whom we preach, warning every man, and teaching every man in all wisdom; that we may present every man perfect in Christ Jesus (Col. 1:26-28).

Powlison describes Wally as a Christian who "loves Jesus Christ" and "believes the Gospel" and desires to share Christ with others" (p. 42). If he is indeed a Christian, why should Wally wallow in his sinful flesh searching for idols when he has been enabled to walk according to His new life in Christ? Perhaps because the clear Bible message has been clouded by Powlison and confused with the worldly psychological methods of self-improvement.

The "old man" is indeed a complex mixture of the evil affects of the world, the flesh, and the devil, but we do not need to analyze it because it cannot be repaired. It had to be replaced. **Sanctification has nothing to do with analyzing and fixing the old man or the flesh. It has to do with walking according to the new life in Christ.** Nevertheless Powlison offers as a method of sanctification his "*process of inner renewal*" (p. 50, italics in original). Next he says,

"Jesus says to take up our cross *daily*, dying to the false gods we fabricate, and learning to walk in fellowship with Him who is full of grace to help us" (p. 50, italics in original). Jesus is speaking of more than "false gods we fabricate." Jesus is speaking about our entire selves. There was no way to save ourselves through any system. Christ, in dying in our place, took our sinful lives with Him and gave us new ones. Indeed, we are to **daily** take up our cross and reckon our old man crucified on the cross with Christ so that we say with Paul, "I am crucified with Christ: nevertheless I live; yet not I, but Christ liveth in me: and the life which I now live in the flesh I live by the faith of the Son of God, who loved me, and gave himself for me" (Gal. 2:20).

Why focus on Wally's problems that relate to his sinful flesh? Why turn all of this into a host of idols? Such a counseling approach will draw people into the flesh rather than into the Spirit. It appeals to the flesh, because the counselee is front and center, explained, and even exonerated to some degree. But believers are not to walk or even change according to the flesh. Why not break the pattern there instead of using psychological pieces of information to detect and dissect the very thing that should be put off (Eph. 4:22)?

Because Powlison's system of sanctification relies so heavily on the wisdom of men about which the Bible warns (1 Cor. 2), it could easily end up being a religion of works whereby one climbs up the ladder of self-improvement, thereby empowering the flesh rather than encouraging true spiritual growth. After undergoing idols-of-the-heart counseling, will Wally truly love the Lord Jesus more? Or, will he become more confident in his management of the idols? Will he become more dependent on Christ or on this new self-knowledge? Will he be growing spiritually or simply strengthening his flesh? Will he become more Christ-cen-

tered or self-centered with this new-found self-knowledge
that requires so much ongoing attention?

If Wally is truly born of God according to John 1:22-23,
his real hope through all of this idols-of-the-heart mess is
that Christ will nevertheless continue His good work in him,
in spite of all this attention given to the fleshly self and a
bunch of idols. We would pray that the very life of Christ in
him would supersede and over-ride this cumbersome idols-
of-the-heart self-effort. Moreover, if the Holy Spirit convicts
him of his sin and he repents and follows Christ, without
referring everything to a particular idol, Wally will find
liberty in Him.

38. Idols-of-the Heart Conclusion

Recycling, reframing, categorizing, and searching for
the "particular pieces of human behavior" in psychology do
not make any of the secular, fleshly origins and practices of
counseling psychology biblical. Powlison may not see that
he truly is an integrationist just like all the rest of them, even
though his approach is beautifully crafted and categorized in
such a way that, when one reads his descriptions of biblical
counseling, one may easily be deceived into thinking that
what he is advocating is truly biblical. Particularly in his
section on "What is the Gospel?" it is clear that Powlison
desires to bring forth spiritual growth through identifying
and dealing with the idols of the heart. Nevertheless, when
he describes the content of the counseling, one sees that his
reframing and what he calls "recycling" end up being filled
with fleshly activities. Counseling that comes forth from
such astute psychological integration will tend to strengthen
the flesh rather than nurture the new life in Christ. One may
admire Powlison's ability to recycle, reframe, categorize,

and describe his system, because he has indeed reached a veritable pinnacle of integration. However, we wonder if his integration might be more dangerous than some of the other forms, simply because his is so beautifully crafted with Scripture and influential argumentation. Yes, his integration might indeed be superior to all others, but then hasn't every Christian integrationist thought he was combining the best from both worlds in the best possible way? Above and beyond all of this idols-of-the-heart counseling mess is the important fact that Powlison's problem-centeredness involves speaking evil about others and is therefore sinful to the core and should be avoided by all believers.

39. Wally in Christ-Centered Ministry

We looked briefly at how one could minister to Bert and Sue through what we call Christ-centered ministry. Part Three gives more information about how one might minister to Bert and Sue and also to Wally through Christ-centered ministry. Here we will consider just a few things to think about regarding how a fellow believer might assist Wally through Christ-centered ministry.

In Christ-centered ministry the person who ministers **would not have to know details about Wally's past or even much about his problems**, since they would not be the focus of ministry. (See Part Three.) There would be no need to analyze Wally to figure out what makes him do what he does and feel what he feels, since Scripture is very clear about the difference between walking according to the Spirit and walking according to the flesh. The focus would be on Christ and the Word of God in reference to Wally. The ministry would be mutual care in the sense that both believers meet at the foot of the cross on equal ground where Christ can minister truth and life to both of them. While there would be teaching and reminding, the one who ministers would endeavor to avoid the pitfalls of one-up/one-down counseling and would certainly never charge a fee for ministering to a fellow believer.

The goal would be for Wally to come to know Jesus Christ more fully as Lord and Savior and as the lover of his soul in the nitty-gritty of daily living. Therefore the person who ministers would strive to nurture Wally's love relationship with Christ and to **help him see how problems of living can be used for spiritual growth.** (See Part Three.) The person who ministers would attempt to guide the conversation towards the ongoing work of Christ in Wally and away from sinful kinds of conversations that are intrinsic to problem-centered counseling as practiced in idols-of-the-heart counseling, as discussed in Part One, and as shown throughout Part Two.

When people like Wally are experiencing the kinds of problems described by Powlison, they need to see their problems from God's perspective. Here problems of living can serve as a wake-up call to walk according to the Spirit rather than the flesh. Therefore the discussion with Wally would involve how the Lord has already worked in his life. Wally would be asked to talk about those times when he turned to Christ and found Him faithful. Wally could relate instances when he experienced confidence in Christ's life in him. We would also want to know about his understanding of the Gospel, his own depravity, the great love of God, the wonder of Christ's death in his place, and the life of Christ indwelling him through the Holy Spirit.

The Bible teaches believers that they have been given new life: "Therefore if any man be in Christ, he is a new creature: old things are passed away; behold, all things are become new" (2 Cor. 5:17). Therefore, **instead of having to learn about all the details of how Wally's "old man" functions**

according to the deceitful lusts, we would give attention to how the new man in Christ functions in Wally. Then Wally will learn to notice whether he is following the sinful ways of the "old man" or the new life in Christ. He will even be able to learn to pick up on early clues of reverting to the flesh before suddenly finding himself expressing more gross aspects of his sinful flesh. The Bible clearly details the differences between the flesh and the Spirit in Galatians 5 and says, "Walk in the Spirit, and ye shall not fulfil the lust of the flesh.... And they that are Christ's have crucified the flesh with the affections and lusts. If we live in the Spirit, let us also walk in the Spirit" (Gal. 5: 16, 24-25).

Rather than learning the idols-of-the-heart system, Wally needs to give more attention to the kind of fruit he is producing. In other words, certain sinful feelings, such as hateful, bitter, envious, or prideful feelings, can serve as a signals that he is walking according to his old life and that he needs to immediately turn to the Lord and repent before he allows his flesh to take him any further into sin. Believers need to practice nipping the old flesh in the bud before it blossoms forth into further sinful talk and actions. If Wally is truly a believer, he has the God-given responsibility and ability to choose to walk according to the Spirit moment by moment. **This is active faith, not any kind of passive piety**. God has given the new life in Christ and thereby the power to choose His way instead of the sinful ways of the old self.

We would talk about what it means to walk by faith, as Colossians 2:6 says, "As ye have therefore received Christ Jesus the Lord, so walk ye in Him." Wally needs to have a clear understanding of the new life he has been given and to learn to walk according to that new life. As a matter of fact, Wally may know all of these doctrines even better than the person who is ministering to him. He may just need to be encouraged to apply what he knows.

Then for those times when Wally reverts to his old sinful patterns, we would want to encourage him to continue to turn to Christ, no matter what. In that way he will learn to see that whenever he reverts to any of his old sinful ways of thinking and acting he is walking according to the flesh rather than the Spirit. We would want to talk with him about all Christ has done for him and remind him that at any point of difficulty he can turn to Christ and walk according to the Spirit. This can be done instantly (often if necessary) through moment-by-moment repentance. 1 John 1:9 reminds believers of the constant availability of shifting from the flesh to the Spirit: "If we confess our sins, he is faithful and just to forgive us our sins, and to cleanse us from all unrighteousness." For the Christian the most prevalent sin is going our own selfish, fleshly way instead of walking according to the new life Christ has given. The more Wally turns and chooses to walk according to the Spirit, the more he will recognize those times when he has reverted to the flesh and will grow in his experience of walking according to the Spirit rather than by the old sinful ways of the flesh.

If Wally talks about his problems, we would ask him what the Lord might be teaching him and how he can apply the Scriptural admonition to be thankful in all circumstances (1 Thes. 5:18). Or, we might ask him how he might use various problem situations for spiritual growth. If Wally begins to complain about his parents or his wife, we would explain that such talk would not be helpful to him and could be harmful, because it may lead to dishonoring his parents and wife and to other forms of sinful thinking and talking. We would not want the ministry time to deteriorate into speaking evil about others. We would ask him to think of those people in a more merciful light and talk about what he can be grateful for regarding his parents and his wife. We might ask Wally to express his thanksgiving to God for the blessings he has received. Beneath all the sinful talk that Powlison described about Wally's parents, one can see that Wally's parents were probably fairly decent, hard working, and conscientious. They obviously wanted the best for their son and it appears that his mother was submissive to his father. **Wally would be better off developing a grateful heart and a merciful manner than sinfully downgrading and dishonoring his parents and wife.**

As Wally finds more for which to be grateful he will see more ways God has blessed him and revealed His love for him. Even in the worst of circumstances one can find things that reveal God's love behind the scenes, even if it is an expression of the Father's love in disciplining His child when necessary. Here it would be thanksgiving for the fact of belonging to God. At all times we would want to encourage Wally to see how much God loves him because it is out of God's love for him that Wally will love God and others, which is the heart attitude of one who is walking according to the new life in Christ as a child of his heavenly Father.

Also, it is vital to remember the presence of the Lord in every situation, whether to comfort or correct or both, whether to encourage or admonish or both, but always to use every situation to conform Wally to the image of Christ and to bring him to maturity. Furthermore, Wally and every one of us need to know God in His fullness rather than through a skewed perspective.

Because Christ-centered ministry is mutual care, those who minister to Wally need to recognize that they can learn from Wally as well as from the Lord during each occasion of providing ministry. Since Wally may indeed have a real heart for souls and for ministry, he needs to be treated as a fellow soldier in the warfare described in Ephesians 6:10-20. We would certainly remind him that he needs to be availing himself of the whole armor of God all the time, since he is on the front line of the battle for souls. In the idols-of-the-heart counseling he is treated as though he is a victim of idols rather than a soldier equipped for battle. If Wally is truly born again, Christ has prepared him for life, service, and warfare. Christ-centered ministry should then serve to strengthen him in the Lord and remind him of all he has in Christ to enable him to walk by faith and to "stand against the wiles of the devil," which can be especially fierce when Christians are about the Lord's business of proclaiming the Gospel and caring for the needy.

It is so easy for those who are in ministry to become so involved in ministry that they neglect their own personal time with the Lord in **daily devotions**, Bible reading, prayer, and worship. (See Part Three.) Just as we emphasize the importance for all believers to be **walking daily** with intentional times of Bible reading, prayer, and worship, we would doubly emphasize that importance for those in full-time ministry and for all believers when they are experiencing problems of living. As mentioned earlier, Part Three gives more details of "What Can Be Done" through Christ-centered ministry

40. CCEF

Problem-centeredness as practiced by the Christian Counseling and Educational Foundation (CCEF) and others in the biblical counseling movement (BCM) draws out and thereby intensifies negative and often angry feelings to the great detriment of the one seeking help. As we reveal throughout this book, such problem-centeredness is both unbiblical and unnecessary. CCEF has a plethora of books on counseling with a great variety of problems of living discussed. We recommend against reading such books if they are problem-centered, because they will discourage many believers from ministering and even exacerbate those problems that are dealt with through such methodology. Problem-centered biblical counselors apparently do not realize that the ones who minister do not need to know people's stories to show them God's glory and their new life in Christ in biblical detail. Therefore, we recommend Christ-centered ministry as we describe in Part Three.

CCEF has a School of Biblical Counseling in which they offer three levels of classes with each one offering a "Counseling Certificate" upon satisfactory completion. One of the ways CCEF has become very much like their secular counterparts in psychotherapy is in their "Counseling Observation." They describe it as follows: "Students observe counseling through a one-way mirror and meet with the counselor following the counseling session."[33] This is a copy of the secular model that is used in various counseling programs at colleges and universities. The people counseled, the counselors, and the observers all know the arrangement, which quickly changes it from private counseling to public performance. Performance? Yes, performance! And some of the "performers" are paying stiff counseling fees while being put on display and being used in this way. This is exactly what happens in the secular setting and surely results in this biblical counseling setting. Moving counseling from the private to the public arena does affect what is said by both the counselee and counselor. At best it superficially represents the problems of the counselee and artificially influences the counseling given.

In our book *Against "Biblical Counseling": For the Bible* we disclose the "Biblical Counseling Compromise" of CCEF (Chapter 5). For example, we say:

Since Dr. John Bettler is in charge of CCEF, he must bear the final responsibility for its integrationist position. Bettler is a member of the North American Society of Adlerian Psychology (NASAP) and a clinical member of the [American Association of Marriage and Family Therapists] (AAMFT). These organizations are purely and simply psychologically oriented groups. The requirements for clinical membership in the AAMFT are extensive and cover four pages in its brochure. We question the wisdom of anyone who is committed to biblical counseling, instead of psychological counseling, being interested in belonging to those two organizations, meeting their requirements for membership, or even attending their conferences.[34]

In a 2003 *PsychoHeresy Awareness Letter* we reveal that several counselors at CCEF have been longtime members of the American Association of Christian Counselors (AACC), Bettler since 6/24/91 and Powlison since 1/11/93.[35] The AACC is committed to the integration of psychology and the Bible. In addition, CCEF has been a fellow traveler with many integrationists through recommending their books or endorsing their work. One in particular that we have exposed over the years is Leslie Vernick.[36] Vernick is a psychologically trained, licensed counselor in private practice, her books are offered by CCEF, and she has taught for them. And, last but not least, is the fact that Powlison endorses Dr. Eric L. Johnson's book *Foundations for Soul Care*, which promotes integration.[37]

In addition CCEF is a separated-from-the-church counseling center that charges a fee for counseling. CCEF current rates are on their web site as follows: "Our basic counseling rate is $85.00 per hour. The initial hour costs $90.00 for set-up fees. **All counseling charges are due before each appointment**" (emphasis theirs).[38]

While the following is dated (2006), nonetheless CCEF's total annual revenues reported then amount to \$2,708,763. This includes all activities of CCEF. However, most of this amount is probably directly or indirectly related to their problem-centered counseling. In 2006 CCEF reported "counseling fees" of \$375,697 and the "biblical counseling" amount at \$399,811, making a total of \$775,508. This one serious violation of Scripture and its pharisaical justification[39] should be enough for all to turn away from the "cash, check or credit card" mentality of CCEF. NANC is not guiltless in CCEF's purveying passion-for-pay plan because Powlison sits as a board member of theirs and the first recommended web site from NANC is the CCEF web site.

"Recycling" or reframing" are mere euphemisms for integration. **The idols-of-the-heart counseling is problem-centered "biblical" counseling psychologized.** Powlison and others at CCEF have made an idol out of idols-of-the-heart and have prostituted "biblical counseling" with the psychological problem-centered wisdom of men and ongoing sinful conversations. **Those at CCEF, while assiduously avoiding pietism, have become guilty of many psychologisms. In summary we say that, contrary to the claims and pretensions of CCEF, they are guilty of psychoheresy.**

41. What To Avoid Conclusion

Prior to the 20th century rise of psychological counseling and prior to the latter part of the 20th century rise of the biblical counseling movement, there was no precedence for an ongoing discussion of such problems as a focus of spiritual growth. We repeat what we have often said about the rise of the psychological counseling movement: the biblical counseling movement, as it is practiced today, would not exist in its present form if it had not been preceded by the psychological counseling movement. As we said earlier, the psychological counseling movement was problem-centered from the very beginning; the biblical counseling movement merely followed this approach.[40] No biblical justification is given by those in the biblical counseling movement for a problem-centered approach. NANC, CCEF, and other BCM organizations are examples of those who indulge in the sinful communication that is produced by problem-centered counseling.

Talking about problems should not be the central content of personal ministry in the Body of Christ. Problems should be seen as opportunities for glorifying God and growing spiritually. Believers need to minimize and generalize talking about problems and maximize and specialize in using problems as reminders to draw one closer to God. Preoccupation with problems and seeking solutions through counseling often inhibit spiritual growth.

Pharisaics?

Someone once explained that the basic position of NANC and CCEF is that the ideal in biblical counseling is one where troubled people receive counseling from their pastor or church family. He said that the separated-from-the-church ministries are not the ultimate model, but, because they are training centers, they are legitimate and can charge fees.[41] One definition of *Pharisaic* is emphasizing or observing the letter but not the spirit of the law.

Both NANC and CCEF would say, "We're not 'the ultimate church sponsored model,' but it's okay because we 'are training centers.'" But, can't any "biblical counseling" center separated from the church be a training center and thereby justify its existence? NANC permits charging and CCEF charges fees for counseling. The fee is justified by virtue of being a "training center."

Whether one is dying in the hospital or "dying" from the sins and heartaches of life, **there is absolutely no biblical reason to charge for ministering to one another in the Body of Christ**. Godly pastors would not stoop to directly charge members of their church for worship services or for private pastoral consultation or for hospital visitation. Godly pastors would not stoop to even suggest or hint at "cash, check, or credit card" for ministry in their church. Nor would they go so low as to attempt to justify charging for worship services and pastoral care by making their church a "training center." Then why dare charge for personal ministry?

Because both NANC and CCEF participate in and support the extracting of money and the degrading of the biblically ordained ministries of the local church, we recommend against both organizations. We think both organizations have drifted too far for too long and are too intertwined to be salvageable.

More Problems

There are more potential problems with nouthetic and idols-of-the-heart counseling than we have indicated, including theological questions and the possible influence of Adams' earlier psychological behavioristic training and Powlison's love of psychology. However, we doubt if any leader in the biblical counseling movement will publicly criticize anything about either approach. Unfortunately the leaders in the biblical counseling movement function somewhat like a good-old-boy network—a mutual admiration society rather than a group of Bereans agonizing for the truth.

Among the greatest detriments to true biblical ministry are the various biblical counseling organizations, including the National Association of Nouthetic Counselors and the Christian Counseling and Educational Foundation. There is an erroneous impression encouraged by such organizations: that one needs to take a biblical counseling course or complete a biblical counseling program before one can competently counsel from Scripture and certainly before one can excel in ministering godly counsel. Therefore, many Christians enroll in these programs with the idea that they need such specialized training before they can or even should minister to another believer. However, the truth is that, for a variety of reasons, one could become a worse counselor after taking such training. For example, one could read their cases and expect to duplicate them in practice. However, no two individuals and no two couples are alike and any attempt to take a case and utilize it as a boilerplate will generally lead to failure.

We say categorically in *Against "Biblical Counseling": For the Bible*:

> Any person who can be used by the Holy Spirit to lead another to salvation or along the way of sanctification is competent to be used by God to give wise counsel without needing specialized biblical counseling training.[42]

It is not the number of books written by Adams or Powlison or anyone else or the number of hours ministering to individuals by them or others. It is not even that one is a theologian or has a pile of degrees and has studied or taught Greek and Hebrew. Mutual care in the Body of Christ happens as the Lord Himself does the major work and the human participants cooperate with what He is doing. **What we say may shock some and be a relief to others**, but it is entirely unnecessary to take classes in order to be effectively used by God to minister godly counsel to one another along the way to Christian maturity.

A disagreement we would have with the biblical counseling training program promoters is that they attempt to prepare individuals to be "biblical counselors," when they should prepare individuals to do biblical ministry as part of the biblically ordained ministries found in Ephesians 4:11-16, Romans 12, and elsewhere in Scripture. One needs to "Study to show thyself approved unto God, a workman that needeth not to be ashamed, rightly dividing the word of truth" (2 Timothy 2:15). Such study occurs in worship services, Bible studies, Sunday school classes, and at other times of reading and instruction in the Word, but is often absent in the biblical counseling movement because of their problem-centeredness.

The biblical counseling movement is a recent phenomenon in church history. The earlier quoted three phases of certification for NANC and the certification program at CCEF **are entirely unnecessary to minister effectively to individuals, couples, and families**. These were not necessary before the invention of the nouthetic counseling system and NANC or the idols-of-the-heart counseling at CCEF, and they are totally unnecessary now. NANC, CCEF, and other biblical counseling organizations act as intimidators and disablers of mature believers who would, with a little encouragement, minister to fellow believers in need. This smacks of the expert/dummy relationship referred to earlier.[43] From our many years of experience, we know that there are numerous Christians who are mature in the faith who would be blessed to minister to others in the fellowship, but who do not because they feel blockbustered by one-up training organizations and educational institutions that promote training followed by more training.

As more and more biblical counseling organizations spring up and as more and more training in biblical counseling is recommended, there will be fewer and fewer mature believers ministering, because they will be more and more intimidated if they have not been trained. **So the idea of more biblical counselors being available by getting more believers trained will actually result in fewer and fewer believers who are mature in the faith ministering to one another in the Body of Christ**. The objective of the biblical counseling training may be to have more individuals available for counseling, but they are discouraging far more people from ministry than they are training, and thus the problem is worsened by the training programs.

The idea of the need for training believers in counseling actually results in believers concluding that they are unable to minister unless they have been sufficiently trained (more and more courses and manuals), supervised, degreed, certificated, and instructed through manuals with contrived counseling cases and special methodologies. In a word, they are intimidated. By shutting down the biblical training programs with their accompanying intimidation, more and more mature believers will begin to minister if encouraged to do so.

Adding to this intimidation are Bible colleges and seminaries that cooperate with NANC, CCEF, or other biblical counseling organizations. **We challenge these institutions that claim to put the Word first to test what we have said according to the very Word they claim to defend. We challenge them to biblically defend the literal detailed dialogues that occur in what is called biblical counseling.** While we are opposed to Christians enrolling in any certificate or degree biblical counseling programs to learn such systems and methods of counseling, **we do encourage those who wish to minister to others to increase their Bible knowledge, to attend Bible classes, or to enroll in a biblical studies degree program rather than a biblical counseling degree program.**

There are numerous biblical counseling books in print and few that have detailed counseling conversations; thus, **we recommend that one withhold judgment about a particular biblical counseling approach until one knows exactly what kinds of conversations go on in the counseling, whether sinful or godly. And note particularly how often or seldom sinful talk and behavior are called "sinful" in their conversations. If such information is not provided, then that should eliminate that approach from consideration. Based upon these many conversations that we have examined over many years, we find that the biblical counseling cases are highly problem-centered and therefore very unbiblical.**

The principles and practices of these two organizations as well as others weaken the position of the church, the role of pastors, the role of church leaders, and even the ability of lay people to minister to one another. Though NANC, CCEF and other BCM organizations contain some good, the church of Jesus Christ is worse off because of the seriousness of their problem-centered counseling.

PART THREE

What Can Be Done

Christ-Centered
Ministry

42. Three Essentials
of Christ-Centered Ministry

Our goal in Christ-centered ministry is to nurture the spiritual life of believers, to equip them to fight the good fight of faith and thereby confront problems of living through exercising faith in Christ and the Word. To do this, the ministry must be Christ-centered rather than problem-centered. To meet this goal both the one who ministers and the one who is receiving ministry will be doing three things: (1) abandoning problem-centeredness; (2) embracing the biblical truth about the role of problems; (3) becoming Christ-centered on a daily basis.

Christ-centered ministry to individuals experiencing problems of living emphasizes the work of Christ in a believer's life. Therefore, the one who ministers needs to keep three things in mind. First, the conversation is to be Christ-centered rather than problem-centered and thus faith-building rather than self-centered. Those who

167

minister will keep in mind such Scriptures as Colossians 2:6-10, "As ye have therefore received Christ Jesus the Lord, so walk ye in him: Rooted and built up in him, and stablished in the faith.... For in him dwelleth all the fulness of the Godhead bodily. And ye are complete in him, which is the head of all principality and power." And, they will **talk about Christ in the believer and avoid problem-centered conversations** with their evil speaking, including gossip, demeaning descriptions of others, blaming the past, playing the victim, and dishonoring parents.

Second, those who minister will remember and teach the biblical truth that for believers problems can be opportunities for spiritual growth: "And we know that all things work together for good to them that love God, to them who are called according to his purpose ... to be conformed to the image of his Son" (Romans 8:28-29).

Third, those who minister will be encouraging fellow believers to walk daily with the Lord: "This I say then, Walk in the Spirit, and ye shall not fulfil the lust of the flesh ... If we live in the Spirit, let us also walk in the Spirit" (Galatians 5:16, 25). Therefore the ministering believer will emphasize the **daily walk**, that is, devoting time each day for prayer, worship, and Bible reading and thereby learning to walk by faith, according to the Spirit rather than the flesh.

The believer who remembers these three elements while ministering to fellow believers will find that, as fellow believers learn to give primary attention to Christ instead of talking about problems, see problems of living as opportunities for spiritual growth, and develop a daily devotional life wherein they learn to walk according to the Spirit, the Lord will provide wisdom for the problems of living.

43. Being Christ-Centered rather than Problem-Centered

A major difference between what biblical counselors generally do and what we recommend is in response to problems of living. The problem-centered counselor finds out what the problem is through conversation with the one in need, who describes the problem in as much detail as possible. Problem-centered counselors are then expected to use their so-called expertise to bring about some kind of change or solution.

Problems are discussed extensively as people expect counselors to solve their problems. This problem-centeredness leads to self-centeredness as the conversation of counseling revolves around the self and its problems. The Bible does not set forth the kind of counseling where two or three people meet to talk about and try to solve one person's (or one couple's or one family's) problems day after day and week after week. We see this in the world of psychological counseling and emulated in much of what is referred to as "biblical counseling."

Instead, God gave Jesus Christ, who is the way, the truth, and the life (John 14:6). God also gave His written Word and the indwelling Holy Spirit. Therefore, we desire to follow His way and His Word as we minister His life. We call this manner of ministry "Christ-centered," because He is the center of the Christian life and worship. He is central to all that is ministered and He is essentially the way of ministry. As in our book *Christ-Centered Ministry versus Problem-Centered Counseling*, our primary thrust here is to encourage Christians to live by faith through giving attention to Christ and His Word rather than on focusing on their problems.

For too long the church has followed the psychological problem-centered approach and we must reverse that tendency, because, for Christians, problems of living test the faith and provide opportunities to grow spiritually and glorify God. On the one hand problems of living tempt many to sin; but, on the other hand, they can motivate believers to turn to Christ and walk with Him according to the new life He has given. Our emphasis is on believers being established in the faith and growing to maturity through all God has provided, by which believers will be enabled to deal with problems in relationship to Christ rather than becoming dependent on a problem-centered human counselor. In other words, we are not called to be problem solvers. We are to be Christ exalters, encouraging those who are beset with problems of living to see trials from God's perspective and to thereby use them for His glory and for their own spiritual growth.

When we speak of problems of living we are talking about the same kinds of problems for which people seek psychological or biblical counseling: personal, marital, and family problems. These involve various aspects of thinking, feeling, behaving, and relating. Each psychological system of counseling has its theory that attempts to describe the nature of man and explain why he does what he does and how he is to change. Each psychological theory involves a secular worldview and a man-centered manner of looking at, diagnosing, and dealing with problems. While the problems of living that plague mankind are common to humanity, there is a vast difference between the way the world views and deals with problems and the way God sees and uses problems for His purposes.

Believers begin their new life in Christ by faith and they are to continue by faith: "As ye have therefore received Christ Jesus the Lord, so walk ye in him: Rooted and built up in him, and stablished in the faith, as ye have been taught, abounding therein with thanksgiving" (Col. 2:6-7). Because believers are to live by faith in God and His Word, their faith is the very thing the enemy of souls will attack through various circumstances and problems of living. Such attacks can both test and strengthen faith. However, if believers become all wrapped up in their problems, they may fail to see that their faith is the object of attack, that it is by faith they are to live, and that it is by faith they will be equipped to overcome temptations to sin when confronted with trials. Since "faith cometh by hearing, and hearing by the Word of God" (Romans 10:7), **the Word must be foremost in thought and conversation in times of trials in order to build one's faith**.

"The just shall live by faith" (Hab. 2:4; Rom. 1:17; Gal. 3:11; Heb. 10:38). Therefore faith in all that Christ has done (to overcome sin, secure salvation, provide new life and power through the process of sanctification, and give believers the solid hope of eternity with Him) constitutes the primary emphasis of all New Testament ministry. However, with the influence of the world and its psychological counseling theories and therapies, people now expect to talk about themselves and their problems when they are in either psychological or biblical counseling.

Therefore, the challenge for biblical ministry is to help individuals move away from self and problems to Christ and what He is working in the believer. Such a change of direction will be contrary to what most people expect. However, encouraging one another to turn to Christ, believe all that the Gospel teaches, walk by faith, pray, and then respond to Him through obedience will nourish spiritual growth. As believers learn to walk by faith in Christ, they will be able to handle their own problems, as most believers who are maturing in the faith already do. Becoming mature in the faith far surpasses any change in circumstances or immediate solutions to temporal problems, though temporal change does accompany spiritual growth. What we are talking about here has eternal consequences, not just solutions that make people feel better for the time being.

Believers Are Equipped to Minister

By God's grace and enabling, believers in the Lord Jesus Christ who are walking daily with Him and maturing in the faith through the trials of life are already equipped to minister to fellow believers who are suffering from the same kinds of problems generally addressed by trained counselors. These believers are equipped to do this by what Christ has already done in them through the Word of God, the work of the Holy Spirit, the trials of life, the fellowship of the saints, and opportunities to serve.

We have come to this conclusion after having examined and rejected the theories and therapies of psychology and after having ministered mutual care in the Body of Christ for over thirty years. Personal ministry is as simple and yet as supernatural as one believer ministering the life of Christ to a fellow believer in whom Christ dwells. The focus is on Jesus, who He is, all He has accomplished for the believer at salvation, and all He is working throughout the believer's sanctification until that day when all believers see Him face to face (1 John 3:2). Therefore those who minister will draw from the "rivers of living water" flowing from the indwelling Holy Spirit (John 8:38-39) and from that which they have hidden in their heart from the whole counsel of God (Psalm 119:11) to encourage fellow believers to turn to Christ for change and spiritual growth. Yet, since they themselves are still in the process of spiritual growth, they will not minister from a position of superiority, but from that of being fellow believers still learning to live by their new life, "which after

God is created in righteousness and true holiness" (Eph. 4:24).

We do not want to intimidate those who are ministering biblically by introducing a new or competing system that must be learned and mastered by those who read it. There is already too much intimidation in the church by those who have developed elaborate approaches to biblical counseling that require courses, certificates, and the reading of many books and counseling cases. We are simply presenting some ideas to complement what others who minister biblically are already doing. We give suggestions on how the one who draws alongside may assist in change and growth with the understanding that God does the primary work and that the person in need has the opportunity and responsibility to follow Him. Some or all of what we present are already being done by those who are not caught in the unbiblical web of psychological integration or the contemporary problem-centered biblical counseling movement as described in Parts One and Two.

We are limiting what we include here, because we are convinced that believers who are maturing in the faith are already prepared to minister to others. In fact, much of what we say will be familiar to those who are already ministering the life of Christ. For those of you who have held back because of intimidation or who have been afraid to move in this direction, we pray that what we say will encourage you to step out in faith, humility, and dependence on God to minister to fellow believers suffering from problems of living and agony of the soul.

We regard what we do and what should be done as *ministry*, not *counseling*. Many in the biblical counseling movement approach counseling with a system of methods and techniques that one must learn and practice. Such systems often lead to a one-up (counselor), one-down (counselee) relationship. (See Parts One and Two.) In contrast, person-to-person ministry of mutual care does not elevate one believer over another, but exalts Christ as the Wonderful Counselor (Isaiah 9:6) and confirms that the Holy Spirit is the indwelling Comforter, who will lead each believer into all truth (John 14:16,17;16:13).

The Bible presents a spiritual ministry for suffering souls: a ministry that centers on Christ and His work in each believer; a ministry that relies on the priesthood of all believers; a ministry that does not involve a methodology of counseling or require specialized training in counseling; **a ministry in which the conversation does not center on self and problems; a ministry that recognizes that trials challenge faith and then uses problems as opportunities for spiritual growth**; and thus a ministry of mutual care and spiritual encouragement in the Body of Christ. All such ministry should flow out of a believer's walk with Christ, according to the Word of God applied in one's own life, and given to a fellow believer in love, mercy, truth, wisdom, and discernment. Rather than depending on a system of counseling, we need to remember Jesus' teachings in John 15:4-5:

> Abide in me, and I in you. As the branch cannot bear fruit of itself, except it abide in the vine; no more can ye, except ye abide in me. I am the vine, ye are the branches: He that abideth in me, and I in him, the same bringeth forth much fruit: for without me ye can do nothing.

What we say in this section should not be taken as a system to follow, but rather as ideas and **suggestions for helping one another to move away from focusing on problems and towards drawing close to the Lord, using problems as opportunities for spiritual growth, and daily walking**

by faith, according to the Spirit rather than according to the flesh.

Above all, we need to remember that Christ is the supreme counselor, that the Holy Spirit is at work in every believer, and that our heavenly Father uses trials both to discipline His children and to conform them to the image of Christ. Even though believers are called and equipped to minister love in mercy and truth to one another, we are nothing more than earthen vessels that the Lord chooses to use for His purposes, so that the power is His and all the glory and praise go to Him (2 Cor. 4:7). When we minister to one another, we need to remember that we are not the prime movers. The real work for both inner and outer change and for any solid solutions that come forth are transactions between the Lord Himself and the one in need.

We pray that every believer will take confidence in what God has provided for living the Christian life and for ministering to one another along the road of sanctification until that glorious day when we will look back on the trials of life and call them a "light affliction" (2 Cor. 4:16). We further pray that all believers will learn to turn to God, look to Christ, and thereby grow spiritually through the trials of life.

Suggestions for Getting Started in Mutual Care

When an individual or couple comes to us with problems of living, we will initially listen to their concerns. However, our first important task is to help individuals stop any evil speaking (Eph. 4:31) about which we warn in Part One and move them to Christ-centeredness. **Moving them to Christ-centeredness, rather than attempting to solve their problems, is central to what needs to be done.** Using Scripture, we may make suggestions or give advice. But, more importantly, we will talk about their faith in Christ and His Word and indicate how God uses problems of living for His children's spiritual growth. We will stress that the best means of dealing with personal and interpersonal problems is through seeking Christ and learning to walk by faith, according to the Spirit rather than according to the flesh. Thus we will emphasize what God has provided for spiritual growth through His Word, the Holy Spirit, and the Body of Christ

Person-to-person ministry may involve some of the same elements as in a regular church service. As people arrive at church, they often fellowship with one another before the service. This gives an opportunity for people to get to know one another better and to encourage one another along the Christian walk. The service itself would include worship, prayer, Scripture reading, preaching/teaching, and announcements of current activities. These are some of the same things that should be going on in personal ministry. One does not need a specific format, but these can be used as a kind of guide. With some individuals, prayer and worship may be the emphasis. With others, teaching and reminding would be central. The "announcements" might be suggestions for becoming involved in some of the activities of the church, suggestions for daily Bible reading and other agreed-upon activities, and arrangements for any future meetings.

Since Christ is the most important and essential Person present during ministry, His presence should be acknowledged. He is the very Creator and Sustainer of the universe ever present as both Savior and Lord. While His presence can always be assumed, purposeful attention and honor are due to Him. Therefore, we would usually begin the ministry session with prayer and worship, thanking God for His presence and coming before Him to receive what He has for each person. We would stress the fact that Christ is there with us and that, since He is uppermost in all of life's circumstances, we will be remembering His very personal involvement during the conversation.

There are situations in life in which people are seeking wisdom and advice regarding personal, marital or family issues. They may simply need wisdom for making certain decisions. If the request is straight forward and not a prelude to introducing other problems of living, a single meeting or a single phone call generally suffices. Seeking this kind of advice would not usually entail those sinful activities about which we warn in Part One. The advice would involve a question and some information related to the question. Such instances would relate more to making a decision than with dealing with those kinds of problems of living generally taken to a counselor. Such questions would generally not be terribly personal. For instance, a couple might ask about what schools would be possibilities for educating their children, or what kinds of discipline might be appropriate for a young child, or how to evaluate a situation at school. Some of these questions might simply be for information about where to purchase some particular items for the family or suggestions on where to move. Or they could be as serious as where to find help for a teenager who has been using illegal drugs. In other words, information and wisdom are sought.

As soon as it is determined that the conversation involves more than ordinary advice seeking, we would proceed with a more general conversation, because we would want to get to know the individual or couple regarding their interests, work, and Christian testimony. We would want to know if they are saved, if they recognize their own proclivity to sin in the flesh, and if they are now living by the new life Christ purchased for them through His death, burial, and resurrection from the dead. If we already know them, we would generally start with what the Lord is doing in their lives. If the individuals in need go into too many details about their problems right away, we would want to move the conversation back to their walk with the Lord and ask what the Lord may be teaching them through the problems they are experiencing. We would aim for a broader perspective, because **believers should be identified by who they are in Christ rather than by their problems**.

Since each person is unique and the Holy Spirit knows what is needed, we would listen, pray, and lean on the Lord and His Word for wisdom. As the person talks about current concerns, we may simply listen and respond with empathy. In seeking to understand, we may ask questions about what was said, being careful to avoid the kinds of sinful conversations about which we warn in Part One. We may comment and even offer some suggestions or advice, when such might be helpful. We would trust the Holy Spirit to bring forth the thoughts, words, and principles from the Word. The one who is ministering should neither feel compelled to make suggestions nor be too quick to give advice. Sometimes the suggestions we make are in the category of what we have learned from the Lord through life experiences and would be optional for the person experiencing the trial. Some of what we might minister would be related to specific and clear Bible teachings that would apply to the situation. However, **ongoing problem solving would NOT be the focus of our ministry**.

One of the great revelations that we came to was that it is not necessary to listen to any ungodly conversation that goes on in most counseling in order to biblically assist those in need. Those who minister need to stop enabling individuals to sin by listening to their sinful talk and, worse yet, asking questions that would lead to more evil speaking (Eph. 4:31). The more the counselor listens to sinful talk, the more sinful talk there will be. Instead, we would talk about God's purposes in trials and how they can be used for spiritual growth, explain that problems attack faith, and communicate that **we want to help equip them to confront their situation by faith in Christ and His Word**. Rather than asking specific questions about their problems, we would ask questions that relate them to the Lord. The following are questions that could be given along the way, but with the idea that some of the questions are more for the person to consider than to answer audibly during the conversation:

What might God be teaching me?

How is my faith being tested?

Do I believe that God can use this problem for His glory and my good?

Is this trial exposing any weak points in my Christian walk?

Is there some "pruning" going on?

How am I being tempted through this trial?

Am I sinning within this problem?

Am I possibly being disciplined by my heavenly Father?

What does He want me to do whether or not the problem is solved?

Do I see this problem as a call to prayer with thanksgiving and worship?

Am I willing to suffer for Christ's sake and for the sake of others?

Am I walking with Christ daily and daily nourishing my walk with Bible reading, prayer, worship, thanksgiving, and service to others when possible?

Or am I allowing TV, sports, concerts, plays, recreation, and other forms of entertainment and self-indulgence to crowd out daily Bible reading, prayer, worship, thanksgiving, and service to others?

These are just a few questions to consider and to give an idea of relating the problem to God's gracious work in the person's life. It might be useful to have such a list of questions on a sheet of paper for the individual or couple to read and consider on their own.

Talking about problems will generally bring a person down spiritually, especially if one is engaged in sinful talk about others, excusing and justifying self, and spending lots of time focused on the problem. Rehashing, reciting, and regurgitating negative circumstances and emotions generally lead to such thoughts and circumstances becoming more imbedded in the mind. Moreover the focus is on self and circumstances, rather than on God and what He might be doing through the problems. We contend that Christ's way through trials and suffering is through daily seeking Him through the Word, prayer, praise, thanksgiving, and worship rather than through weekly rehashing problems in an effort to fix them. Therefore mutual care would minister encouragement and instruction regarding the daily walk. A person can gain far more by going to the Word and praying to the Lord than by talking about problems with another individual. **That is why talking about problems needs to be replaced with talking about the Lord and His promises and provisions, going to the Word, praying, worshipping the Lord, and encouraging a consistent daily walk.**

Drawing Believers to Christ-Centeredness

Probably the greatest challenge of moving into Christ-centered ministry is the usual preoccupation with problems and with describing and discussing them in detail. The idea of finding help through talking about oneself and about one's problems is firmly embedded in the minds of most Christians. **Therefore moving away from problem-**

centeredness is one of the most difficult tasks in Christ-centered ministry. In fact one measure of progress will be that problem-centeredness will fade away and the time will be devoted to spiritual matters. When people become immersed in problems, they often begin to walk by sight instead of by faith. They lose hope. They cannot see God's love in the midst of the trial and thereby they revert to the flesh. They need encouragement regarding Christ's presence, care, involvement, and enabling as they seek to follow Him through difficult circumstances. Drawing their attention back to Christ encourages faith, hope, and love.

What are the means of drawing believers to be Christ-centered in all that they do and especially when encountering problems of living? They are the same means that have been given to every believer since the Day of Pentecost: the Word of God empowered and applied by the Holy Spirit, worship, prayer, the fellowship of the saints, and service. It depends on trusting God to do the essential inner work. **It is not one of probing for details about the person or the problem.** While we avoid probing for details about the problem, we are concerned that fellow believers are suffering and therefore desire to point them to Christ, who is the "Wonderful Counsellor" (Isaiah 9:6); to the indwelling Holy Spirit as our constant helper; and to our heavenly Father, who uses trials both to discipline us and to conform us to the image of Christ.

Because of the usual fixation on problems and the compulsion to fix them, there must be a concerted effort to draw attention to God Himself. People will almost always drift back into the direction of talking about those problems. At each point along the way the ministering believer may respond with empathy and compassion, but always with the idea of redirecting the attention to God—His purposes, promises, truth, authority, and especially His great love. If people are only looking for immediate solutions, they will miss the great opportunity to know Christ better and to grow spiritually.

In turning the conversation back to Jesus and His provisions for spiritual growth, the ministering believer should not force or use pressure if the individual resists this ministry. Jesus also met with resistance when the people were looking for a king to give them physical bread rather than a savior who could give them new life (John 6:25-66). Jesus did not change His plan or succumb to giving them what they wanted rather than what they needed. Some followed Him; others went away. Those who minister must continue to be faithful to the Lord and His Word so that they can say with Paul:

> Now thanks be unto God, which always causeth us to triumph in Christ, and maketh manifest the savour of his knowledge by us in every place. For we are unto God a sweet savour of Christ, in them that are saved, and in them that perish: To the one we are the savour of death unto death; and to the other the savour of life unto life. And who is sufficient for these things? For we are not as many, which corrupt the word of God … (2 Cor. 2:14-17).

Not all people will be willing to go the way of Christ—the way of spiritual growth through the problems of living. They may try to force the ministering helper into the role of counselor and expect him/her to listen to all the details and to solve the problems. Or they may simply look for someone else who will fill that role. This does not mean that the ministering believer has failed. The responsibility is to minister truth in love and mercy and to be faithful to the Lord and His Word. Some who want a different kind of help may not return. Others may keep coming back but make no progress. In such cases ministry may have to be discontinued, especially if there is ongoing sin and rebellion against the truth that has been set forth by the ministering believer. On the other hand, those who will catch the vision of what God has for them in Christ-centered ministry will grow in their spiritual walk and they will become equipped to help others. There will be great joy and thanksgiving observing the glorious changes that can happen as faith flourishes and love abounds, even in the midst of problems as the Lord works in and through circumstances.

Avoiding the Pitfalls of Becoming Problem-Centered

It is very easy to get into the trap of problems. People expect to solve their problems by talking about them week after week, month after month, and, for some, year after year. That focus is unbiblical! It is not only problem-centered; it is self-centered. The person with the problems becomes the center of attention and continues to be the center of attention as long as problem-centered counseling continues. In fact, some people like this relationship of having problems that someone else must solve. In Christ-centered ministry, as problems are brought up, the direction of ministry must be to encourage the individual to seek the Lord and use the situation as an opportunity to know Him better.

Another pitfall to avoid is spending time talking about the past. This takes the eyes off Jesus, communicates the idea that present behavior is determined by past circumstances, shifts blame for sin, and tempts people to dishonor their parents. The past can neither be changed nor fixed. One may encourage another to confess the sins of bitterness and unforgiveness to the Lord, but the details do not need to be discussed. Regarding the past, the apostle Paul said, "but this one thing I do, forgetting those things which are behind, and reaching forth unto those things which are before, I press toward the mark for the prize of the high calling of God in Christ Jesus" (Phil.3:13,14). There is no example in Scripture of anyone being led back into their past for emotional healing from past offenses. Believers are new creations in Christ and are to press forward in sanctification until Christ has completed the good work in each one.

Every person has both sinned and been sinned against. In fact, some people have been grievously sinned against and we do not want to minimize or ignore that fact. Nevertheless, healing does not come from focusing on the pain that others have inflicted. If that were the case, there would be a great deal of attention given to that in the New Testament, since many First Century Christians would have been victims of pagan sexual perversions and of the exploitation of slaves.

A prevailing idea from psychology, embraced by many, is that those who have been sinned against need to be healed from their emotional pain before they can progress with the Lord. Actually such a psychological mindset is a deceptive trap where the focus of being emotionally wounded by others takes precedence over the recognition of one's own sin. God's answer for all problems of living is the cross of Christ and the new life He gives. As believers recognize the ways they have sinned and continue to sin against God and others, they see God's great love in mercy and truth. As they reckon themselves to be dead unto sin and alive in Christ (Romans 6:5-11), they will see that the old reactions to having been sinned against actually reside in the old ways of the flesh that are to be put off and reckoned dead. **Those who give more attention to God's great forgiveness of their own sins than to the sins other people have committed against them are able to move ahead in their Christian walk in love and gratitude.**

Diverting from Talking about Problems

Talking about problems in counseling often involves various forms of sinful communication, such as talebearing, speaking ill of one's spouse or others, blaming the past, playing the victim, and dishonoring parents. (See Parts One and Two.) There are many other forms of self-centered and sinful communication, but we use these five faults of problem-centered counseling to show what can be done. Diverting away from such self-centered communication will not only help curtail sinful talk but will also redirect attention to Christ.

Because people have become accustomed to the idea that one must air problems in order to get help, they will easily slip back into that mode even after one has explained the importance of being Christ-centered instead of problem-centered. Therefore, we give a few brief examples of what might happen and what can be done. While each section emphasizes one of the five deadly dangers of problem-centered counseling—talebearing, speaking ill of others (such as in marriage counseling), blaming the past, playing the victim, and dishonoring parents—they often accompany one another. **Though not specifically mentioned in all of the following brief descriptions, the biblical role of problems in a believer's life will be taught.** The goal in each is to direct attention to Christ and to how He can use the very trials believers may be suffering to bring them to maturity. These examples will be given in the feminine gender, since women are the ones who usually seek counseling, as discussed in Part One.

Diverting from Problem-Centered Talebearing

Sarah begins by explaining that she and her sister, Maria, are now responsible to take care of their elderly mother, since they are their mother's only children. She continues,

"Maria and I do not get along. All we do is argue and I end up doing almost all the work. She criticizes the way I do things and even complains to our mother that I'm not doing what I should be doing. Our poor mother is caught in the middle because Maria says all kinds of bad things about me behind my back." The usual problem-centered counselor would begin to ask questions and to seek information on the whys and wherefores of this problematic relationship.

In contrast, the Christ-centered helper would begin by reviewing the difference between problem-centered counseling and Christ-centered ministry and then might say something like this: "This may sound a bit divergent, but since you will find real help for your situation in Christ and since we want Christ to be central in our conversation, let's begin by talking about Him." Next, the one who ministers would ask questions to find out Sarah's understanding of salvation. If Sarah leaves out the doctrine of the depravity of man, there would need to be some teaching and/or reminding about how depraved every person's flesh is and thus the dire need for salvation and also about the warfare between the flesh and the Spirit within every believer. The Christ-centered helper may also review what Christ did on the cross to give each believer new life in Him (Romans 6-8). She may ask Sarah, to describe what it means to her to have Christ living in her.

This kind of conversation provides a new perspective on the problem at hand, because remembering that Christ is living in us makes a huge difference in our relationships with others. The other people, including her sister, may not change, but Sarah has God-given means for change and growth. At this point the Christ-centered helper may talk about Sarah's present problems as opportunities for spiritual growth and ask something like this: "What might the Lord want **you** to do to improve your relationship?" In response Sarah might think of something that she could do that would both please the Lord and help the situation. However, she might respond by saying, "My sister and I are complete opposites. She calls me a goody-goody because I'm pretty straight compared to her. All she cares about is how cute she is and how she wows the men with her flirting and with all the you-know-what." This would be another opportunity for a problem-centered counselor to find out the details of "you-know-what" and to spend lots of time talking about this relationship without Maria present and with great possibilities of talebearing. In contrast, the Christ-centered helper could respond with the following: "Since Maria is not here right now, why don't we talk further about your walk with the Lord and how this might help you in your relationship with your sister." As Sarah grows in her walk with the Lord, she will learn either how to get along with her sister or learn how to live with the difficult situation in a godly manner.

When a woman we'll call **Jane** comes for help and says she is miserable at work because people don't treat her right, the usual problem-centered counselor would probe for details and suggest solutions that may or may not be helpful, or, if the counselor suspects that there are some deep-seated reasons within the person, the probing might go in that direction. The Christ-centered helper would want to find out about Jane's understanding of salvation and what it means to be "in Christ," for if she sees circumstances from God's perspective she will be able to use these problems as opportunities for spiritual growth and have a greater realization of His involvement with her at the workplace. The Christ-centered helper might ask what blessings has He bestowed there and how has He enabled her to cope with the situation or revealed anything to her about her own sinful flesh.

One can also go to various places in Scripture to remind Jane that Christians have been foretold that they may not be treated right, even when they are doing what is right. Jesus said that the world would hate His followers (John 15), the apostle Peter talked about how believers are to respond to unjust treatment (1 Peter 2), and the apostle Paul demonstrated throughout his ministry both the temporal and eternal value of suffering for the sake of the gospel (2 Corinthians 4). In other words, Jane's walk with the Lord, her testimony for Christ by her demeanor, and her opportunities for spiritual growth are far more important than talking about how miserable she is at work. Someone might argue that, if Jane talks through the details of her problems at work, the counselor might be able to help her find ways to get along or even encourage her to quit that job. We contend that, if Jane draws close to the Lord and begins to see things from His perspective, she herself will find what might be done. One who ministers biblically may also help Jane find ways to get along or make other changes, but from a different perspective.

Diverting from Problem-Centered Speaking Ill of Others

In Parts One and Two we gave numerous details about what goes on in marital counseling. If a wife, husband, or couple seeks help, the usual problem-centered counselor will want to know all kinds of details about the marriage. The ensuing discussion will both allow and elicit much verbal violation of Ephesians 5:22-33 regarding the husband loving his wife and the wife reverencing her husband. What might a Christ-centered helper do when complaints are aired? If only the wife has come for help and she begins complaining about her husband, a question such as the following could divert the conversation away from him and back to her own walk with the Lord: "Could this situation be used to mature you in the faith?" The Christ-centered helper may also talk about how marriage can be a blessing in more ways than people often think, and one of the ways it can be a blessing is this: the difficulties can be great opportunities for spiritual growth. Here we have two people rubbing against each other and God can use this to conform His children unto the image of Christ (Romans 8:28-29). If the woman has come for help, she can be the one to change and grow, even if she thinks her husband is the one who needs to change.

If both the husband and wife come to a Christ-centered helper, it would be helpful to say near the beginning of the meeting that, since we are meeting together to edify one another, it would be good to think a moment about Ephesians 5:33, "Nevertheless let every one of you in particular so love his wife even as himself; and the wife see that she reverence her husband." Then if they begin to speak poorly about one another, the Christ-centered helper might say something like the following: "You are both in a perfect place for spiritual growth, and I'm speaking about more than just your relationship with one another. You can each take advantage of the difficulties you are experiencing with one another for your own spiritual growth." Then the Christ-centered helper could spend a few minutes teaching about how God uses suffering for one's benefit and even for His glory. The Christ-centered helper could then minister truths of the gospel to help them see who they are in Christ and what He is doing in each of them individually.

Diverting from Problem-Centered Blaming the Past

Because so much problem-centered counseling looks into the past for the whys and wherefores of today's problems, people expect to talk about the past. In fact, many blame their present problems on their past. The horrible healing of memories fad has led too many Christians to believe the all-pervasive myth that they need to be healed from wounds from the past before they can get on with living the Christian life. Most problem-centered counselors will explore the individual's past to some degree. In contrast, the Christ-centered helper will attempt to keep the conversation in the present and in view of the future glory God has in store for His own. Talking about the past would be limited to one who might be seeking the Lord regarding any personal responsibility to others that could be fulfilled in the present. The past that would be emphasized by the Christ-centered helper would be remembering and talking about what the Lord has done in the person's life from the time she was born again until the present. Any reference to the past having to do with blaming the past and looking for past explanations for present problems would generally involve talebearing and faulty memory. Therefore the Christ-centered helper would attempt to divert the conversation away from blaming the past.

Nancy said her life totally changed after a particular man wooed her and wowed her and then kept her hanging and waiting and wondering for several years until he finally dropped her. The usual problem-centered counselor would want Nancy to describe what happened and how she felt and then explore ways in which these things changed her thinking, feeling, and acting. Instead of going in that direction, the Christ-centered helper would gently explain that there is no need to talk about the past because it cannot be fixed or changed and that there is no need to understand how it might be affecting her today, since all that would be limited to speculation.

Instead, the Christ-centered helper would begin by exploring Nancy's understanding of salvation. She might ask such questions as, "What has Christ done for you?" "Why did he have to die in your place?" "Do you believe that without Christ having died in your place you would be lost?"

"What does the new life in Christ mean to you?" "How can you live that new life in Christ today?"

The Christ-centered helper might explain that the enemy of our souls wants to keep people living according to the old ways of the flesh and one way is to keep them looking backwards by blaming the past. Since, the Christian is called to be looking in the other direction, the Christ-centered helper might ask the person to read Hebrews 12:2, "Looking unto Jesus the author and finisher of our faith; who for the joy that was set before him endured the cross, despising the shame, and is set down at the right hand of the throne of God"; 2 Corinthians 3:18, "But we all, with open face beholding as in a glass the glory of the Lord, are changed into the same image from glory to glory, even as by the Spirit of the Lord"; and Philippians 3:13-14, "Brethren, I count not myself to have apprehended: but this one thing I do, forgetting those things which are behind, and reaching forth unto those things which are before, I press toward the mark for the prize of the high calling of God in Christ Jesus." In Christ there is hope for today and for the future.

Joyce said that her uncle had sexually abused her all through her elementary school years and that she still had "flashbacks." Again, the problem-centered counselor would probably explore this and all of the possible ramifications in trying to help Joyce. In contrast, the Christ-centered helper would not probe but would divert the conversation by asking Joyce about her walk with the Lord and by continuing with much of what was discussed regarding the past in the prior example. But, in addition, the Christ-centered helper would suggest that Joyce use the "flashbacks" as a signal to turn to the Lord and to thank Him for giving her new life in Christ and to remember that what happened to her cannot touch her relationship with Christ or His life in her (Romans 8:31-39). In other words, Joyce would be using the flashbacks for her own spiritual growth until they fade away or simply continue to be useful calls to prayer. The Christ-centered helper might ask Joyce to regularly meditate on Galatians 2:20, "I am crucified with Christ: nevertheless I live; yet not I, but Christ liveth in me: and the life which I now live in the flesh I live by the faith of the Son of God, who loved me, and gave himself for me," and to think about how this verse relates to her daily walk.

Diverting from Problem-Centered Playing the Victim

While there are true victims, the psychological mindset, which has gripped both our culture and church, has turned nearly everyone into a victim, primarily a victim of often exaggerated, past maltreatment by parents, other people, and circumstances. Even true victims do not do well as long as they dwell on their victimhood or even see themselves as victims. However, as some observers have noted, playing the victim is a very prevalent but damaging way to avoid responsibility and blame others. Some who seek help truly see themselves as victims and have lived as victims for some time. Problem-centered counselors generally think they need to hear the details in their attempt to help these people overcome their painful past or be "healed" from their "wounds." In contrast, Christ-centered helpers will attempt to divert the conversation away from all the talk that leads to or expresses a victimhood mentality and will therefore turn the conversation to the One who is victorious in overcoming evil.

We know a woman who was in a horrible fiery car crash in which she lost an arm, an eye, and the skin from her face and elsewhere on her body. She is a true victim and people would understand if she felt sorry for herself. However, Christ has obviously done a miraculous work in her life, because she not only manages to take care of herself well, but is also out serving others. Because of Christ, her compassion for others supersedes preoccupation with her own circumstances. That same miraculous life is available to every Christian, because it is the very life of Christ indwelling the believer through the Holy Spirit. But how do we encourage a fellow believer to move away from seeing herself as a victim? Again, we would take the person to the cross and ask questions regarding salvation, the new life in Christ, and what that new life means. We would want to be both gentle and direct as we ask questions similar to those we asked Nancy (above).

Julia insists that she can't help the way she is because of the way she was shunted off to boarding schools during most of her growing up years. Even after we have explained much of what was said to the others about blaming the past, she keeps on insisting that not being treated properly while she was growing up has made her miserable and was the cause of her two divorces and is the reason her own children do not want to be around her. Julia would be quite a challenge for anyone to help because she seems immovable. Problem-centered counselors could spend weeks and months trying to help her by talking about her childhood, her failed marriages, and the problems she has with her children. In fact, if Julia likes problem-centered counseling, she could be a paying client for years to come.

In contrast, a Christ-centered helper may lose Julia unless she is willing to follow Christ. Each time, Julia turns back to seeing herself as a victim of parents and circumstances, a Christ-centered helper will remind her, "Julia, if Christ is truly living in you, you have a new life to live today. You do not have to be a victim of your past or even of present circumstances. But, I wonder if the Holy Spirit may be gently bringing to mind something that you might have done wrong yourself. If so, you can take it to the cross right now and confess privately to the Lord according to the promise of 1 John 1:9, 'If we confess our sins, he is faithful and just to forgive us our sins, and to cleanse us from all unrighteousness.' I don't need to know what it is or what you might be praying, so I'll just wait quietly while you do business with God." **A Christ-centered helper would not always take this approach, but we include it here to show how the ministry time should allow times of quiet reflection and personal prayer to the Lord without the one who is ministering having to know the sin or the content of the prayer.**

Betty was quite exasperated when she came through the door exclaiming, "I can't believe how everyone takes advantage of me and then they don't even appreciate me, no never!" She pauses a moment and then says, "And not only that. They complain about how I can't do anything right." Ooooh! This covers a lot of territory, a whole lifetime of being taken advantage of, not being appreciated, and then being criticized for not doing anything right. This is more than ample fodder for a problem-centered counselor to dive into. Without bothering to correct her "always" and "never" statements of exaggeration, the Christ-centered helper would gently take her to the cross and minister truth in love. Oh! The wonders of what Christ has done! His great love for the downtrodden! His great care of even the sparrow! His thorough knowledge of Betty and all she has suffered and His plan to work mightily in her for His glory and her good!

Christ-centered personal ministry of care, comfort, burden bearing, encouragement, exhortation, instruction, and admonition is to draw one's attention to Christ Himself so that the one with the problem may be spiritually equipped to trust and obey Him through every trial. Our emphasis is on faith building through praying together, reading the Bible together, reminding one another about the truths of Scripture, worshipping God, and fellowshipping together.

As problems come up we hope to direct attention away from them as quickly and gently as possible. We will speak about the Gospel wherein is great power, about the new life Jesus has given every believer, and about who He is, what He has done, what He has revealed about Himself in His Word, and where He is leading. We will encourage a daily pattern of diligently seeking the Lord through the Word, prayer, praise, worship, and thanksgiving.

Diverting from Problem-Centered Dishonoring Parents

Wanda began by talking about how much she was growing spiritually, especially since she had joined a book study she was in, where she learned why she had turned to drugs and alcohol when she was a teenager. She excitedly said that she was finally dealing with her childhood and she was getting healed from all kinds of pain she did not even know was there. The only problem, she said, was that she had been feeling very depressed over the past few weeks. Most problem-centered counselors would be very interested in what she had learned about her past in their attempt to help her overcome her depression. In contrast, a Christ-centered helper would be more interested in hearing about her spiritual past. Had she been born again by having placed her trust in Christ through the preaching of the Gospel? The ministering believer would want to have some understanding as to whether Wanda understood the Gospel and truly believed or if it was simply an emotional response without understanding.

She asks Wanda what her spiritual walk had been like before she started this book study? Wanda confesses that it was not that great and proceeds by exclaiming that she now realizes that all her present problems stem back to her parents who didn't really love her, that during her childhood her mother cared more about having a nice clean house than on spending special time with her, and that her father had substituted real love with all the expensive things he bought for her. Again, the typical problem-centered counselor would probably explore the details of the childhood and throughout the counseling there would be much discussion about her parents and their mistakes and failures. Throughout all of this Wanda would be breaking the commandment to honor parents and would actually be doing harm both to herself and to her parents by speaking ill of them and blaming them for her problems.

The Christ-centered helper could proceed with the following plan. She could say that it's wonderful that Wanda desires to grow spiritually and that is exactly what Christ-centered ministry is all about. She could then talk about how God can use problems in a believer's life for good and then explain that dwelling on and talking about problems, whether in the past or the present, tend to bring one down, but that looking up to Christ in faith and trust can lift one up to the light of truth and freedom from sin and guilt. The Christ-centered helper might then ask Wanda about her own use of the Bible, prayer, worship, and service to others. If Wanda is not consistent here, the helper could encourage her in that direction. Then, since it is clear that Wanda has been dishonoring her parents, the one who ministers might suggest that together they read and discuss God's promise in Ephesians 6:2-3: "Honour thy father and mother; which is the first commandment with promise; That it may be well with thee, and thou mayest live long on the earth."

The ministering helper might mention that ruminating about unhappy events in the past, dwelling on problems, and blaming parents can actually be very depressing. She may further say that spiritual growth does not come as a result of thinking about the sins of others but by looking unto Christ and all He suffered to bring salvation and forgiveness, by loving and thanking Him, and by confessing one's own sin (1 John 1:9). Information could also be given about memory, how it changes through time, how it can be colored by present thinking, and how it can be distorted and altered by suggestions from others and even from reading certain books. In fact, the Christ-centered helper might even suggest that Wanda discontinue the book study group and start thinking about ways she might have sinned against her parents while she was growing up and about things about her parents for which to be grateful.

But what if Wanda had been severely abused by her parents? Would there be a different way? Each person is unique and the conversation would be different, but the same principles would apply; the same moving away from the problems of the past, away from blaming others, and away from excusing one's own sins; the same turning to Christ, the Gospel, and the biblical way of using trials for God's glory and spiritual growth; and the same encouragement to follow Christ daily.

Caring for One Another's Soul

Jesus calls us to love one another even as He has loved us (John 15:12). Other Scriptures urge us to bear one another's burdens (Gal. 6:2) and care about one another's concerns (Phil. 2:4) with an attitude of meekness and humility (Phil. 2:3). We would desire to give the very sympathy and supporting encouragement to our brothers and sisters in their trials as we would desire in ours. As we come alongside, we do so with the understanding that our brethren in Christ are suffering attacks to their faith and that our response, as members of the same body, is to strengthen and encourage.

All caring for one another in the Body of Christ must be centered in Christ's love, expressed in both mercy and truth. While there are general admonitions in Scripture as to how we are to treat one another, each of us has our own manner of conversing and relating. In fact, the flow of the conversation will depend on the persons involved, the circumstances, and the topics discussed.

While outward concerns are not ignored, Christ-centered ministry is more concerned with the condition of the soul. As mentioned earlier, there are similarities between the biblical counseling problem-centered approach and the Christ-centered ministry approach. Both care about the soul, but the emphasis is different. As we consider the soul, we recognize that some individuals tend to emphasize head knowledge while others emphasize the emotions. Through knowing and following the Word and responding to all that Christ has done, both the mind and the emotions work together with the will. God's love flowing through the person works together with faith and desire based on the truth God has revealed in His Word. Therefore, rather than only presenting a Scripture directly related to the problem, we would want to emphasize those sections of the Word that explain the spiritual possibilities in trials and that would stimulate gratitude, faith, and love for God and for one another. God has given believers a renewed mind to know, understand, and believe His Word; a heart to love Him with a desire to please and serve Him; and a will that is affected by both.

Another similarity between the biblical counseling problem-centered approach and Christ-centered ministry is that both deal with salvation and sanctification. However, quite often the problem-centered approach involves so much talking about the problem that one's eternal destiny may not be clearly established and the process of sanctification may possibly be replaced by external compliance accomplished in the flesh. We would want to emphasize salvation and sanctification and the role of trials in both.

We would want to make sure that those seeking help have a clear understanding of the cross of Christ and an ongoing gratitude for God's most precious gift. We would seek to minister the Gospel to those who may only be professing Christians and not truly born-again believers. Some professing Christians have an incomplete understanding of redemption, why it was necessary and all it entails. Even faithful church attenders may have no real understanding of salvation or of their great need for what Christ accomplished on Calvary, especially if they are blind to their own human depravity. As we discuss these essential truths, we would present the Gospel, which is life-sustaining to genuine believers and life-producing for unbelievers and for those who might be nominal rather than genuine believers.

A great deal happens when people are saved. Their sins are washed away, totally and completely. They are both born again by the Spirit and adopted into the family of God. The Holy Spirit comes to live in them to guide and direct them in their new life. They are rescued out of the kingdom of darkness and translated into the kingdom of God. While they will continue to sin when walking according to the flesh, they are no longer under the domination of sin, for they have a new Lord and a new life in the Spirit. They begin a personal relationship with God that is more intimate than any other relationship can be, since God lives in them through the Holy Spirit. They are under His constant care and can communicate with Him at any time. They are spiritual beings as well as earthly beings and have begun a whole new adventure with God. From this point on they are in the process of sanctification until they are glorified with Christ. Personal ministry is to encourage ongoing sanctification, which is truly an inner work that the Holy Spirit works in each individual through the Word of God received, believed, and obeyed by grace through faith.

Encouraging the Believer's Love for Christ

When people are overwhelmed by problems they often lose sight of God's love for them. They need a glimpse into Romans 8:28-39 to remember that God's great love cannot be diminished or destroyed, even by dire circumstances. Nothing can separate His love from His children. The apostle Paul prayed for believers to "comprehend with all the saints what is the breadth, and length, and depth, and height; and to know the love of Christ, which passeth knowledge, that [they] might be filled with all the fullness of God" (Eph. 3:18-19). It is out of this great love relationship that the new life flows. Therefore Paul continues his prayer with these words, "Now unto Him that is able to do exceeding abundantly above all that we ask or think, according to the power that worketh in us" (Eph. 3:20).

As believers grow in knowing God's love through the clear teachings of Scripture, they will grow in their new life and will thereby be able to face various trials in the Spirit rather than according to the flesh. They will be able to surmount problems even if circumstances do not change. When attention is given to the magnificent love relationship that God has given every believer in Christ, there is a great opportunity for gratitude to flow and for the desire to do His will being kindled. The true Christian life is marked by love for God and one another and by gratitude, thanksgiving, praise, and worship even in the deepest trial. When obedience flows out of love and gratitude, it will not deteriorate into the works of the flesh motivated by earthly desires. Obedience that is an expression of love nurtures the spiritual life, but obedience for fleshly gain will merely sow to the flesh and "of the flesh reap corruption" (Gal. 6:7-9).

Because the flesh can act in seemingly godly ways and even follow God's law to some degree, there is always the possibility for external obedience after the flesh. The Pharisees present a clear picture of this ability of the flesh to appear godly. Jesus saw their hearts and accused them of being hypocrites:

> Woe unto you, scribes and Pharisees, hypocrites! for ye make clean the outside of the cup and of the platter, but within they are full of extortion and excess. Thou blind Pharisee, cleanse first that which is within the cup and platter, that the outside of them may be clean also. Woe unto you, scribes and Pharisees, hypocrites! for ye are like unto whited sepulchres, which indeed appear beautiful outward, but are within full of dead men's bones, and of all uncleanness (Matthew 23:25-27).

The fleshly motivation for change could be for outward results, such as appearing good before others or having a "marriage that sings." (See Part Two.) That kind of motivation can lead to fixing behavior in response to rewards and following commands through external behavior without the transforming work of the Holy Spirit in the heart. External change accomplished too easily in the flesh can lead to hypocrisy and pride. It can even become a subtle source of increasing the power of the flesh and diminishing a person's dependence on the Lord.

Biblical counseling often encourages obedience in order to solve problems or improve a situation. Christ-centered ministry encourages people to have a greater realization of what God has already done for them and to love Him through obedience by grace through faith. The First Epistle of John explains how our love for God and one another comes from God's love for us. "Herein is love, not that we loved God, but that he loved us, and sent his Son to be the propitiation for our sins" (1 John 4:10). Christ-centered ministry would emphasize the vertical relationship out of which the horizontal should flow. Biblical counseling is often on the horizontal plane, using Bible verses regarding the problem and how it might be fixed, with the vertical (the powerful relationship with God) being secondary or simply assumed rather than emphasized. We contend that the vertical must be given primary attention—the focus must first be on Christ.

Living by grace through faith in Christ is a life that is wholly and daily dependent on Him, as He works through the Holy Spirit according to His Word. While many would say, "Yes, of course, that is to be assumed in all that we do," the redemptive relationship is often simply assumed, rather than addressed, and therefore receives secondary rather than primary attention. Yet, Paul spent three chapters in his letter to the Ephesians on that essential relationship before exhorting them to "walk worthy of the vocation wherewith ye are called" (Eph. 4:1), before describing the kinds of behavior that should flow out of the new life. Therefore, we would encourage believers to give much attention to this life-giving and life-sustaining relationship and to nourish their inner life in the Spirit on a daily basis.

Some professing Christians have a shallow view of salvation because they have an inadequate view of how sinful and rebellious all humans are in the flesh, including themselves. In overlooking, or excusing or justifying their own sinfulness they do not fully comprehend the extent to which Christ went for them in dying in their place. Many have been so focused on the sins of others that they have failed to see their own sinfulness and therefore have failed to grasp the fullness of Christ's love. The result is not only weak faith, but also less love. When Jesus went to the home of Simon the Pharisee, "a woman in the city, which was a sinner, when she knew that Jesus sat at meat in the Pharisee's house, brought an alabaster box of ointment, and stood at his feet behind him weeping, and began to wash his feet with tears, and did wipe them with the hairs of her head, and kissed his feet, and anointed them with the ointment" (Luke 7:37-38). When Simon complained, Jesus asked him which of two debtors would have greater love for the creditor who had forgiven their debt. Simon answered correctly: the one with the greater debt. Jesus then said to Simon:

> Seest thou this woman? I entered into thine house, thou gavest me no water for my feet: but she hath washed my feet with tears, and wiped them with the hairs of her head. Thou gavest me no kiss: but this woman since the time I came in hath not ceased to kiss my feet. My head with oil thou didst not anoint: but this woman hath anointed my feet with ointment. Wherefore I say unto thee, Her sins, which are many, are forgiven; for she loved much: but to whom little is forgiven, the same loveth little (Luke 7:44-47).

In other words, those who don't see their sinfulness "love little" and those who recognize, repent, and have received forgiveness love much. When people grasp a greater comprehension of their own past depravity and the current sinful proclivity of their flesh, they will gain a greater understanding of how much God has forgiven them and they will love Christ all the more. In most cases, human depravity and sin should be taught generally, rather than the one who ministers digging for specific sins to address. It is far better when people are convicted by the Holy Spirit than by a mere human.

As believers respond to God's love for them, their love for Him will grow. When they truly love Him, they will desire to do His will. As they walk in His love by grace through faith, the Holy Spirit will enable them to love and obey Him more and more. Therefore all personal ministry should nurture that love for God in response to His great love. The essence of the Christian life is love for God and love for others. The one who is growing in knowing the love of God that passes understanding and who is growing in loving God with all his heart, soul, mind, and strength and his neighbor as himself will mature in his ability to withstand the worst of life's difficulties.

44. Recognizing the Biblical Truth about the Role of Problems

Since the way we view problems will influence our course of action, believers need to think seriously about God in relation to every problem of living, not just to seek a solution, but to seek God Himself. We hope to help believers direct their attention away from self and problems and towards the Lord Himself as He creatively works in His children through the challenges and trials of life for His glory and their good.

The world sees problems as impediments to accomplishments, progress, and happiness. The idea is to get through problems and solve them as soon as possible so that one can get on with life. The Bible presents an entirely different perspective on problems of living and even on the most horrendous trials. Therefore, we would want to help fellow believers gain a biblical perspective on their own circumstances and problems of living so that they can rightly respond and benefit from whatever trials, afflictions, and problems of living they are experiencing. We would want them to realize that trials attack faith and test it and that trials can be used to strengthen faith and foster spiritual growth. As problems occur in the lives of His children, God is able to accomplish a far greater feat than we can ever imagine as He uses them to conform His children unto the image of Christ (Romans 8:28-29).

The Bible begins with God's perfect creation of all that exists, including humans created in the image of God, and then reveals the disastrous source of all problems: rebellion against God, first by Satan and his minions, next by Adam and Eve when they ate the forbidden fruit, and then followed by their sin-infested progeny, generation after generation. Problems of living, therefore, are not isolated human events of grief and disaster, but part of the spiritual battle that has been raging throughout the ages. The Bible is the true story of mankind's sin and rebellion, of God's wrath against sin and His love for mankind, and of His eternal plan for reconciliation through Jesus Christ. The Bible reveals how much every person needs the Savior, both for initial salvation and then for ongoing spiritual growth until the magnificent fulfillment of being conformed to the image of Christ and of being with Him eternally.

According to His eternal plan and wisdom, God uses mankind's challenges, trials, and sufferings to reveal His glory, to show forth the nature of man, to expose sin, to draw people into relationship with Himself through the Gospel, and to bring forth spiritual growth in His children. Throughout Scripture God used trying circumstances to accomplish His purposes, and He uses problems of living in the lives of believers today. Those in whom Christ dwells can be confident that their own problems are not without some good purpose.

Many purposes are fulfilled through trials that work for the good of believers. However, trials in themselves are not necessarily beneficial; it is what God works in the believer through the trials and it is also how the believer responds to God in the midst of those trials. The same trial may afflict two different people, with one turning to God in faith and the other one blaming other people, circumstances, and even God Himself. Obviously one leads towards God and the other away from God. Therefore as believers experience trials we desire to encourage one another to trust God to use them for good.

Problems of living can be like torn up ground in one's life wherein the Lord's Word can be sown and watered. They can be the very means by which the Lord gets one's attention and reminds the believer about abiding in Him through trials and following His Word by walking according to the Spirit. God uses problems to expose sin for the purpose of repentance, forgiveness, change, and spiritual growth. God also uses suffering to refine His children into "pure gold" and to glorify Himself (1 Peter 1:7). He will use suffering to correct and discipline. Yet, not all suffering is the result of a person's own sin. The apostle Paul suffered greatly because of his faithfulness to preach the Gospel. Nevertheless, whatever the source of suffering, all can be used to show forth God's glory as believers choose to depend on Him and to follow Him in all circumstances.

Using Problems of Living
as Opportunities for Spiritual Growth

Christ-centered ministry sees problems as opportunities to know Christ more fully, love Him more deeply, and follow Him more completely. Problems of living can serve a wonderful purpose when people turn to the Lord and seek Him above all else. Moreover, turning to the Lord during such times enables believers to gain wisdom from His Word as the Holy Spirit enlightens the mind and brings forth applications in the life. Indeed, trials, problems of living, and suffering are often those times in which the greatest spiritual growth occurs. When ministering we often begin with these truths so that the believer's attention is redirected to the Lord of the universe. In Christ there is a new perspective and hope regarding His purposes and possibilities in the trial, wherein the believer has opportunities to glorify Him, be strengthened in faith, and become spiritually equipped for the future. We thus inject the hope He gives, which is even beyond what the believer might be anticipating, because of the opportunity of growing in the knowledge of Him who "is able to do exceeding abundantly above all that we ask or think, according to the power that worketh in us" (Eph. 3:20).

The way of spiritual growth that God has planned for every believer is not problem-free. Instead, God uses everything for the ultimate good of His children. Indeed, as Paul wrote after having endured excruciating trials, "Though our outward man perish, yet the inward man is renewed day by day. For our light affliction, which is but for a moment, worketh for us a far more exceeding and eternal weight of glory" (2 Cor. 4:16,17). The individual who follows this course will be walking with the Lord, learning to put on Christ, gaining wisdom, building faith, practicing obedience, and growing in his relationship to the Lord—all of which will equip him for life and service, as well as for dealing with present and future problems. The Holy Spirit will be doing the significant work in the believer.

Treating Problems of Living as Trials with a Purpose

Rather than becoming immersed in problems of living and looking mainly to get rid of them, we want to encourage believers to **treat problems of living as trials with a purpose**. Preachers over the centuries encouraged believers to have confidence that God uses believers' trials and sufferings for His glory, including the spread of the Gospel, and for their good. This view often gets lost. In fact, **we know of no organized biblical counseling approach that emphasizes the spiritual usefulness of trials while diverting away from focusing on problems of living**. Nevertheless, we see how the Bible shows forth God's purposes being fulfilled through afflictions and agonizing circumstances. The Bible also urges people to look to God and His Word rather than focusing on the problems themselves and speculating the whys and wherefores of the problems and proposing solutions that may be man-based.

The Book of Job reveals God's purposes in human trials that show forth His glory and wisdom and demonstrate the power of faith in God. After the devastating loss of his children and all his possessions, Job's response was "Naked came I out of my mother's womb, and naked shall I return thither: the LORD gave, and the LORD hath taken away; blessed be the name of the LORD." And the Bible further says, "In all this Job sinned not, nor charged God foolishly" (Job 1:21-22). Then after Satan afflicted him with painful boils all over his body, Job's wife said, "Dost thou still retain thine integrity? curse God, and die."

Job answered "Thou speakest as one of the foolish women speaketh. What? shall we receive good at the hand of God, and shall we not receive evil?" The Bible further says, "In all this did not Job sin with his lips" (Job 2:9-10). Job's faith was being tested to its fullest; yet, there was the further test: the conversation and focus on Job's problems. Above all and throughout all of the talk about his problems, their supposed cause, and what he should do, Job tenaciously held onto his integrity and his faith in God. Yes, he complained grievously, but he looked to God to set things straight. Job kept his faith, proved Satan wrong, won the spiritual battle, and received great rewards at the end. But when he saw God's glory, he was overwhelmed and said, "I have heard of thee by the hearing of the ear: but now mine eye seeth thee. Wherefore I abhor myself, and repent in dust and ashes" (Job 42:5-6).

The Book of Job demonstrates the disastrous consequences of human speculation when it comes to problems of living and problem-centered counseling. The reader is shown from the beginning that Job's problems originated from Satan, but only as permitted by God. In their ignorance and arrogance, Job's problem-centered friends sought to discover the source by considering their own observations of other cases and cruelly added admonishment and blame to Job's grievous loss and excruciating pain.

Every problem is on the larger landscape of spiritual warfare where our "adversary the devil, as a roaring lion, walketh about, seeking whom he may devour" (1 Peter 5:8) and where "the flesh lusteth against the Spirit, and the Spirit against the flesh" (Gal. 5:17). Seeing the bigger picture does not entail giving undo attention to the devil, but rather recognizing that Jesus won the victory on the cross and enables believers to resist the devil with the shield of faith, the Word of God, and prayer (Ephesians 6). Therefore, ministry in the Body of Christ is to encourage one another to stand firm in faith and to walk according to the Spirit: "Walk in the Spirit, and ye shall not fulfil the lust of the flesh" (Gal. 5:16).

While the devil doesn't make us do it, he does all he can to undermine the faith of believers through problems of living, and by getting people focused on themselves and their problems, and through the accompanying temptations to sin. Every trial contains a temptation to turn from God and seek what seems best for self. Therefore, every trial must be seen as a call to spiritual arms and to remember that God is the supreme authority, who is able to use trials for good.

Those who are experiencing problems of living may have no clue as to the real source of their problems, which may be their own flesh and/or spiritual wickedness in high places (Eph. 6:12). They may be struggling against circumstances and other people instead of donning their spiritual armor, standing firm in faith, and praying. The apostle Paul urged believers to look beyond the obvious in his letter to the Ephesians:

> Finally, my brethren, be strong in the Lord, and in the power of his might. Put on the whole armour of God, that ye may be able to stand against the wiles of the devil. For we wrestle not against flesh and blood, but against principalities, against powers, against the rulers of the darkness of this world, against spiritual wickedness in high places. Wherefore take unto you the whole armour of God, that ye may be able to withstand in the evil day, and having done all, to stand. Stand therefore, having your loins girt about with truth, and having on the breastplate of righteousness; And your feet shod with the preparation of the gospel of peace; Above all, taking the shield of faith, wherewith ye shall be able to quench all the fiery darts of the wicked. And take the helmet of salvation, and the sword of the Spirit, which is the word of God: Praying always with all prayer and supplication in the Spirit, and watching thereunto with all perseverance and supplication for all saints (Eph. 6:10-18).

As believers turn to Christ and all He has provided for fighting the good fight of faith, they will better know how to handle problems. They will thereby be glorifying God and fulfilling His purposes. Yes, there are biblical admonitions for what people can do about certain specific problems and we would minister those when appropriate. However, believers need to see the larger picture through the great doctrines of Scripture so that they will follow God rather than self, circumstances, or Satan.

Problems of living and other trials and afflictions perform a tremendous work in every believer. After writing about the glories of salvation: "being justified by faith," having "peace with God through our Lord Jesus Christ," having "access by faith into this grace wherein we stand," and rejoicing in "hope of the glory of God" (Rom. 5:1-2), Paul went so far as to say that he gloried in tribulations:

> And not only so, but we glory in tribulations also: knowing that tribulation worketh patience; And patience, experience; and experience, hope: And hope maketh not ashamed; because the love of God is shed abroad in our hearts by the Holy Ghost which is given unto us (Romans 5:3-5).

Many people long for experience with God and they seek all kinds of exciting manifestations, but experience with God often comes through trials. It is when our faith is tested that we find God's faithfulness to His Word. The truth of the Gospel we believe is confirmed over and over again in the trenches of daily life. Each test of faith can drive a believer deeper into the Lord as the shield of faith fends off the fiery darts of doubt and condemnation. Especially in our culture of instant this and one-minute that, waiting on God in the midst of trials both tests and strengthens patience. Looking unto Jesus brings the hope that is established in truth. Moreover, as we experience the truth of God's Word through trials we grow in our personal knowledge of His love so that His love is indeed shed abroad in our hearts and out to others.

Suffering brings us into that close intimacy with God wherein we taste of Christ's suffering and also of His great consolation as he comforts us. Thus we are enabled to con-

sole others with the consolation we have received from
God.

> Blessed be God, even the Father of our Lord Jesus
> Christ, the Father of mercies, and the God of all com-
> fort; Who comforteth us in all our tribulation, that
> we may be able to comfort them which are in any
> trouble, by the comfort wherewith we ourselves are
> comforted of God. For as the sufferings of Christ
> abound in us, so our consolation also aboundeth by
> Christ (2 Cor. 1:3-5).

The word *comfort* includes compassion and caring, but it
also means encouragement and even exhortation as the literal
meaning of the Greek word means "a calling to one's side."[1]
Therefore this is a very personal, close relationship type of
caring that would be strengthening as well as comforting.
The primary relationship is with our God of all comfort as
believers draw close to Him through all trials and establish a
daily walk of diligently seeking Him by grace through faith
(Heb. 11:6). The secondary relationship is between fellow
believers as they minister from what God has already given
them.

Believers are not to ask for trials or instigate problems
for the sake of spiritual growth. However, trials can serve
to make hardy believers, accustomed to the storms of life,
as they are being strengthened in faith, developing patience,
maturing in every spiritual discipline, and bearing much fruit
for God's kingdom and glory. In fact, trials accomplish so
much that James says:

> My brethren, count it all joy when ye fall into div-
> ers temptations; Knowing this, that the trying of your
> faith worketh patience. But let patience have her per-
> fect work, that ye may be perfect and entire, wanting
> nothing (James 1:2-4).

Trials test the faith and reveal whether or not it is genuine. They also reveal areas of unbelief. If we resist trials and murmur and complain, we will not benefit from them. But, if we turn to God in faith, trusting that He will use them for our spiritual growth, then we will benefit far more than we realize at the time. Notice that as believers become patient through trials by trusting and obeying God, they will become mature and lack nothing because they will find that they have all they need in Christ.

Trials are not joyous in themselves, but difficult and often painful and even long-lasting. The joy comes from the prospect of God working His perfect will in His children through the trials. It is the kind of joy that Jesus knew during the greatest suffering of all, for it was "the joy that was set before him" (Hebrews 12:2). The joy was in the anticipation of completing the requirements for our salvation, the anticipation of much fruitfulness, as when He told His disciples, "Except a corn of wheat fall into the ground and die, it abideth alone: but if it die, it bringeth forth much fruit" (John 12:24).

For believers the joy comes through faith in God's promises, that He will accomplish good and that these trials work an "eternal weight of glory," as Paul declared:

> For our light affliction, which is but for a moment, worketh for us a far more exceeding and eternal weight of glory; While we look not at the things which are seen, but at the things which are not seen: for the things which are seen are temporal; but the things which are not seen are eternal (2 Cor. 4:17-18).

Remember that what Paul calls his "light affliction" included all of the afflictions, persecutions, great physical pain, and much overall suffering that he lists in the eleventh chapter of 2 Corinthians:

> Of the Jews five times received I forty stripes save one. Thrice was I beaten with rods, once was I stoned, thrice I suffered shipwreck, a night and a day I have been in the deep; In journeyings often, in perils of waters, in perils of robbers, in perils by mine own countrymen, in perils by the heathen, in perils in the city, in perils in the wilderness, in perils in the sea, in perils among false brethren; In weariness and painfulness, in watchings often, in hunger and thirst, in fastings often, in cold and nakedness. Beside those things that are without, that which cometh upon me daily, the care of all the churches (vv. 24-28).

Paul knew that his calling as a Christian was to endure suffering for the sake of the Gospel. As days darken in our circumstances, we need to follow Paul's example of knowing our calling as believers and to use all circumstances for the sake of the Gospel, the glory of God, and our own growth to maturity in Christ. If we are thinking more about Christ and His call on our life than our own feelings and desires and as we turn to Him, He will bring us through and cause us to be victorious in Him. At the same time He will use the trials to produce patience, perseverance, maturity, spiritual hardiness, and skill in using the shield of faith and sword of the Spirit. Trials prepare us for further trials that may come, particularly persecution.

The Bible tells us that Jesus "was in all points tempted like as we are, yet without sin" (Hebrews 4:15). Every problem we face carries a temptation with it and Jesus was tried to the uttermost so that He can both sympathize with us in our trials and strengthen us through His very presence and power, for He is ever making intercession for us. Therefore, as we go through the trials of life we need to be looking unto Him.   Jesus was tried to the utmost, not only in temptation but also in much opposition and suffering. He went through much affliction and suffering beyond all other human beings and He did it to procure our salvation by suffering the eternal punishment for all our sins on Calvary. In dying in our place He also gave new life in Him, peace with God, and power over sin. Nevertheless, He did not remove the presence of sin and the inevitability of problems, trials, and suffering. He clearly told His disciples to expect them (John 15). Instead of removing problems and trials, Jesus uses them for His glory and our good, and He has given us all we need for life and godliness, even in the most trying circumstances.

After describing the horrendous trials of Old Testament saints, the letter to the Hebrews urges believers to endure suffering by looking unto Jesus.

> Wherefore seeing we also are compassed about with so great a cloud of witnesses, let us lay aside every weight, and the sin which doth so easily beset us, and let us run with patience the race that is set before us, Looking unto Jesus the author and finisher of our faith; who for the joy that was set before him endured the cross, despising the shame, and is set down at the right hand of the throne of God. For consider him that endured such contradiction of sinners against himself, lest ye be wearied and faint in your minds. Ye have not yet resisted unto blood, striving against sin (Hebrews 12:1-4).

Jesus endured the suffering "for the joy that was set before Him": that He would bring many sons to glory.

Many of His children, however, suffer from problems of living because they need His chastening and discipline.

They need reproof, correction, and training in righteousness. Therefore the writer to the Hebrews reminds us:

> My son, despise not thou the chastening of the Lord, nor faint when thou art rebuked of him: For whom the Lord loveth he chasteneth, and scourgeth every son whom he receiveth. If ye endure chastening, God dealeth with you as with sons; for what son is he whom the father chasteneth not? (Heb. 12:5-7).

In His great love for us He does all this "for our profit, that we might be partakers of his holiness" (Heb. 12:10). This is not punishment for sin, but rather chastening unto righteousness: "Now no chastening for the present seemeth to be joyous, but grievous: nevertheless afterward it yieldeth the peaceable fruit of righteousness unto them which are exercised thereby" (Heb. 12:11). Therefore, when believers realize that some of their problems are due to their own sin, they have hope. They know that they have a Father who loves them enough to bring the right correction and they have a Savior who has paid the full penalty of all their sin—past, present, and future—and He gives us the privileged access and invitation to go directly to Him whenever we sin: "If we confess our sins, he is faithful and just to forgive us our sins, and to cleanse us from all unrighteousness" (1 John 1:9).

Turning to Christ and looking at Him through His Word and to Him in prayer will bring spiritual growth if the person desires Christ more than a change in circumstances or immediate solutions to the problems. Does the person desire God and His will enough to spend time daily seeking Him and growing in Him? If the person truly desires God's perspective, God's will, and God's work on sanctification through the problems, there will be spiritual growth and God's enabling to deal with both current and future problems. With the right perspective on problems, instead of being bogged down and preoccupied with them, people will learn to lean on Christ, trust Him, and follow Him through each circumstance.

Worshipping God through the Trials

When Christians who are growing spiritually experience various trials and turn to God and worship Him, they gain a greater vision of God and a biblical perspective on their problems. In doing so they find Him faithful. The apostle Paul found God's grace fully sufficient to the point that he said, "Therefore I take pleasure in infirmities, in reproaches, in necessities, in persecutions, in distresses for Christ's sake: for when I am weak, then I am strong" (2 Cor. 12:10). Such people handle difficult circumstances as they turn to God and follow Him. They see the glory of God working through and in the midst of trials and they give Him the honor and glory due Him.

David endured many trials and the Psalms are full of calls to worship. In Psalm 102 David cries out to the Lord in his affliction, wherein his "heart is smitten, and withered like grass" and he has "mingled [his] drink with weeping." But then he considers the greatness of God and begins to worship Him when he says, "But thou, O Lord, shalt endure for ever; and thy remembrance unto all generations." Here he exalts the Lord in his smitten heart. He gets a larger perspective and is able to endure and face whatever God has next for him.

Worship both prepares believers for facing problems of living and gives them the right perspective when trials come. Just as worship is of supreme importance in public gatherings of the church and is the most blessed time in private devotions, so too must worship be the primary emphasis when believers minister to one another in difficult times. **This worship can be done through praying together, talk-**

**ing together about Jesus, thanking Him, singing or read-
ing Psalms and hymns, reading portions of Scripture
together, sharing ways Jesus has worked in the past, or
listening to sermons.** These elements of worship should take
precedence over the problems themselves, and an attitude of
worship should prevail as believers are encouraged to trust
Jesus to work His will in each situation.

When people worship God during trials, they not only
recognize His ability to help; they also acknowledge His
wisdom, submit to Him, and seek Him regarding what He
wants them to do. However, some people are so used to cen-
tering their attention on problems and wanting others to fix
them that they may not want to "waste time" doing spiritual
activities. They may not see how worshipping Christ could
possibly help with the problem at hand. Many would see this
as simply a distraction and would fail to see the application.
Moreover, the flesh only knows how to deal with problems
according to carnal means and the devil encourages the
works of the flesh as he uses problems of living as strong-
holds against the knowledge of the Lord.

**Therefore, we encourage all who are undergoing
any kind of suffering to turn that suffering into a call
to worship daily.** In worship believers will find Christ's
sufficiency and the grace and spiritual strength to endure.
In worship they will rise above the battle, glorify God, and
obtain a victory that can only be gained through prayer,
adoration, and worship. While they do not see God with their
human eyes, they will see Him in spirit so that they will be
able to say with Job, "I have heard of thee by the hearing of
the ear: but now mine [spiritual] eye seeth thee." They will
bow in humble adoration and be ready to walk through the
circumstances according to Christ's life in them and thereby
according to God's purposes for them.

Ministering and Remembering
God's Word through the Trials

When we talk about ministering to people we actually mean that we are ministering the Word, empowered by the Holy Spirit. **Therefore we do not need to understand people or to understand their problems specifically.** The Word, ministered by the Holy Spirit, will transform lives, which is something the ministering believer cannot do.

Jesus Himself is the very Word of God made flesh and therefore when believers minister Christ, they will minister according to the written Word of God, which is quick and powerful. It is life-giving, life-sustaining, and life-changing:

> For the word of God is quick, and powerful, and sharper than any two-edged sword, piercing even to the dividing asunder of soul and spirit, and of the joints and marrow, and is a discerner of the thoughts and intents of the heart (Heb. 4:12).

The Word has power to give life through the Gospel and to work sanctification in the believer. The Word can reveal truths to a person about himself that no one else knows. It can "reveal the thoughts and intents of the heart" to encourage the fearful, convict the sinner, strengthen the weak, humble the proud, and make other major changes on the inside. Therefore God's Word is like a living textbook because the Holy Spirit works in and through it to nurture the new life in Christ and to enable believers to love, trust, and obey Him.

Believers are called to:

> Study to show thyself approved unto God, a workman that needeth not to be ashamed, rightly dividing the word of truth. But shun profane and vain babblings:

for they will increase unto more ungodliness" (2 Tim. 2:15-16).

Therefore those who minister to others will devote time to the Word. They will read, study, and compare Scripture with Scripture. "Rightly dividing the word of truth" is letting the Bible interpret itself rather than using the wisdom of the world to explain it away. That is why Paul warns Timothy to "shun profane and vain babblings," because they will distort the understanding of the pure Word of God. *Profane* actually means "of the world" and *vain babblings* would be useless or unhelpful talk. Much counseling is of the world and is based on theoretical speculation and unhelpful talking aimed at fixing up the self, which is, in reality, the "old man" that is to be reckoned dead according to Romans 6:6. Therefore, when people try to integrate psychological theories and therapies with the Bible they are distorting the true meaning of God's Word and bringing in useless speculation and talk.

Besides reading and obeying the Word of God, those who minister should rely on it. The Bible is both inspired and authoritative. Therefore, what it says is far more valuable than anyone's opinion or personal experience. It is from God Himself, as He chose to reveal truth to mankind through chosen men who would communicate His revelation (2 Peter 1:19-21). Furthermore God says that His Word will do what He plans for it to do, for He says: "So shall my word be that goeth forth out of my mouth: it shall not return unto me void, but it shall accomplish that which I please, and it shall prosper in the thing whereto I sent it" (Isaiah 55:11). Notice that the Word will do what God purposes, not what humans may want it to do.

Mutual care should always include encouragement for believers to be reading the Word for themselves. The Word actively changes lives as believers attend to it and follow what it says.

> All scripture is given by inspiration of God, and is profitable for doctrine, for reproof, for correction, for instruction in righteousness: That the man of God may be perfect, thoroughly furnished unto all good works (2 Tim. 3:16-17).

This verse is an amazing promise. Notice that the Word brings believers to maturity so that they are equipped to serve God with good works. Biblical doctrine, along with reproof, correction, and further instruction, establishes them in the faith both in knowledge and obedience. The Word does so much more than any human helper can do. Therefore, one goal of ministry is to encourage fellow believers to read and apply God's Word in their lives every day.

Because "all Scripture ... is profitable for doctrine, for reproof, for correction, for instruction in righteousness," the one who ministers is not restricted to those verses that appear to address specific problems, but may select other Scriptures, such as those that address aspects of God's character or the particular uniqueness of the individual in specific circumstances. It may be that a particular believer needs a clear understanding of what it is to walk according to the new life in Christ before specific verses dealing with behavior are applied. Otherwise the person may outwardly conform according to the flesh. Of course, if there is clear sin, it can be identified by Scripture (reproof) and then both doctrinal teachings and corrective verses may be applied. Thus personal ministry will consist of teaching or reminding one another about what the Bible teaches regarding "instruction in righteousness."

The training of believers who will minister is that very training in the Word that the Lord supplies to all believers as they read His Word and seek to follow Him through life's adversities. They do not have to have degrees or certificates, but they should be on-going learners and doers of the Word. They will be living and ministering according to Colossians 2:6-10:

> As ye have therefore received Christ Jesus the Lord, so walk ye in him: Rooted and built up in him, and stablished in the faith, as ye have been taught, abounding therein with thanksgiving. Beware lest any man spoil you through philosophy and vain deceit, after the tradition of men, after the rudiments of the world, and not after Christ. For in him dwelleth all the fulness of the Godhead bodily. And ye are complete in him, which is the head of all principality and power.

Notice that the Christian life is to be lived on the same basis as salvation itself, by grace through faith. God Himself gives them the grace to walk by faith in Him and in His Word. Believers are to be "rooted and built up" in Jesus and "stablished in the faith," which means being established in the faith (the doctrines of Scripture). This is not faith in faith, but faith in God and in His Word.

As believers sink their roots deep in Him and His Word and become solidly established in the faith, they will grow in knowing the Word, following Christ, and "abounding therein with thanksgiving." They will be enabled to do so even in the midst of severe trials, because they will know that no matter what happens to them, these essential doctrines of the faith will never change. God's Word is an anchor to the soul and holds firm even in times of agony.

Next comes the warning to avoid those who live by and minister according to the ways of the world rather than according to the Word of God: "Beware lest any man spoil you through philosophy and vain deceit, after the tradition of men, after the rudiments of the world, and not after Christ" (Col. 2:8). "Spoil" in this context means to rob, steal, or plunder. Has the believer's full confidence in Christ been spoiled or eroded? Have any been robbed of the peace that the world does not give? Perhaps a fellow believer has been spoiled "through philosophy and vain deceit after the tradition of men, after the rudiments of the world, and not after Christ." Philosophy in this context could be any worldly way of looking at life, a worldly perspective, or a worldly mindset in contrast to looking at life according to His life and His Word. It is a mind set on self rather than on Christ.

"Vain deceit," like the old snake oil deceitfully touted to give all kinds of benefits, refers to empty promises that the world makes and that the devil has made from the beginning. These are especially dangerous when the vain deceit is made to sound holy and Christian, but is a mixture full of "the tradition of men, after the rudiments of the world, and not after Christ." Elsewhere in Scripture, Paul warns about the wisdom of men in contrast with the Word of God (1 Cor. 2:4-6). When believers abandon such wisdom of the world as the theories and therapies of psychological counseling, they are not left empty-handed. They have Christ, the Living Word of God! Colossians 2:9-10 clearly states why believers should be following Christ instead of the traditions of men and the rudiments of the world: "For in him dwelleth all the fulness of the Godhead bodily. And ye are complete in him, which is the head of all principality and power." What worldly system can even touch the wonder of all that is in Christ? He is completely God and believers are "complete in Him." Notice how this sentence ends by saying, "He is the head of all principality and power." So there is no reason to turn to the world for issues of life and godliness when believers experience problems of living. Jesus clearly said: "If ye continue in my word, then are ye my disciples indeed; And ye shall know the truth, and the truth shall make you free" (John 8:31-32).

There is more power, wisdom, healing and help in any truth from Scripture than from all the psychological theories and therapies conceived by those who devised or utilize the nearly 500 different systems of psychotherapy. Therefore, believers need to know the Word. Some may have been taught what they need to know but have not applied the teaching to their present circumstances or even their lives. Therefore, the ministering believer will be both teaching and reminding fellow believers about what the Word says. As Paul advised Timothy,

> If thou put the brethren in remembrance of these things, thou shalt be a good minister of Jesus Christ, nourished up in the words of faith and of good doctrine, whereunto thou hast attained (1 Tim. 4:6).

45. Becoming Christ-Centered on a Daily Basis

Encouraging a Daily Walk

Since the biblical way through suffering and trials is by walking with the Lord on a daily basis, a primary goal of personal ministry should be to encourage one another in walking daily with Him. This daily walk involves thinking, feeling, deciding, and doing in reference to the Lord. It is very easy to drift into walking according to the ways of the fleshly self in thoughts, desires, plans, and purposes. People may even be doing what is moral, but acting according to the life and effort of the flesh rather than according to their new life in Christ.

Most people with problems are preoccupied with their problems daily and even moment-by-moment. This is the time when the world, the flesh, and the devil and the lust of the eyes, the lust of the flesh, and the pride of life often take over. **Every day is a battle with the flesh and that is why believers are to remember their spiritual armor and use their spiritual weapons every day.** Each trial can serve as an excellent reminder to turn away from the world and turn to Christ daily. James 4:8 tells us to "Draw nigh to God, and he will draw nigh to you." We would want to help fellow believers establish a daily walk with the Lord in their thinking as well as in their praying, worshipping, reading Scripture, and following the Lord in faith and obedience. Christians who are in the midst of problems cannot afford to be Sunday-only Christians.

Jesus said, "Man shall not live by bread alone, but by every word that proceedeth out of the mouth of God" (Matt. 4:4). Jesus also explained to His disciples: "My meat is to do the will of him that sent me, and to finish his work" (John 4:34). Indeed, spiritual nourishment comes from God's Word and from doing His will. Daily nourishment is essential for spiritual growth and for meeting the challenges of life. Therefore, we encourage fellow believers with problems to make a plan for daily devotions and involvement in the local body of believers through faithful attendance and service. Rather than prescribing what the person should do, we make suggestions, such as the following: daily personal Bible reading, memorizing Scripture, listening to preaching and teaching (including church services and classes, tapes, CDs, MP3s, DVDs, and internet sermons), praying, fellowship-ping, serving others, reading devotional books and articles, worshipping, singing hymns, or writing one's testimony. Some people may, in addition, find that they draw close to the Lord when they are exercising personal creative gifts such as painting, drawing, singing hymns, writing songs, or writing poetry or essays. Simply going for a walk in God's wondrous creation can be spiritually invigorating, especially when thinking about things for which to be grateful.

For these activities to be of full spiritual benefit, there needs to be a deepening desire to know God more fully and to follow Him more completely. Faith and diligence bring reward: "But without faith it is impossible to please him: for he that cometh to God must believe that he is, and that he is a rewarder of them that diligently seek him" (Hebrews 11:6). As one truly seeks the Lord daily, He will reveal Himself through His Word, show the way, and enable the believer to do His will by grace through faith. When the believer reads the Word and listens to sermons, the Holy Spirit can direct behavior and enable the person to change without another human telling him what to do or how to change. In this way the person becomes equipped for the trials of life and learns to walk in dependence on the Lord rather than depending on other people to set him straight or advise him on what to do next.

Prayer is a great privilege for believers and is especially essential when experiencing trials. Our Father hears every prayer as the Holy Spirit intercedes for us when we pray (Romans 8:26-27) and as our Lord Jesus is our mediator ever interceding for every believer. Prayer is so vital for the Christian walk that the Scriptures instruct us to "pray without ceasing" (1 Thes. 5:17). God thus commands us to do that which is the very best for us. He calls us to communicate with Him daily and often, even to pour our hearts out to Him as David did throughout the Psalms. **How much time is squandered stewing, worrying, and mentally rehashing problems instead of taking them directly and immediately to God in prayer!** How much better to talk to God about what is on the heart and disturbing the soul! Prayer brings close communion and fellowship and it puts the mind and heart into a powerful dependence on God.

> Be careful for nothing; but in every thing by prayer and supplication with thanksgiving let your requests be made known unto God. And the peace of God, which passeth all understanding, shall keep your hearts and minds through Christ Jesus (Phil. 4:6-7).

God has provided some excellent examples to follow in prayer that can be suggested for daily devotions. The greatest example, of course, is the Lord's Prayer, recorded in Matthew 6:9-13 and Luke 11:2-4. The apostle Paul's prayers for believers are also filled with examples of how and what to pray for one another. We would suggest becoming familiar with the prayers in Ephesians 1:17-23, Ephesians 3:16-19, and Colossians 1:9-17 to pray accordingly for one another. Many of the Psalms are prayers as well.

Personal ministry occurs for a brief time compared to the many hours that believers can spend in fellowship with Christ. Every believer has the opportunity to walk daily with Christ, who is available 24/7 through the indwelling Holy Spirit. The daily walk is where Christians can mature and especially when there is a deep desire to know Christ better and to follow Him more faithfully. As believers develop a daily devotion to the Lord they will be spiritually strengthened for enduring the trials of life and they will also be in a place of gaining spiritual understanding and wisdom for how to handle difficult circumstances. **This should be a constant, ongoing teaching in the church and an ongoing encouragement for all believers.**

Beginning with Daily "Lite"

The goal of a daily walk may be new to some people. Those who are not accustomed to reading Scripture and praying on a consistent daily basis may feel overwhelmed by "one more thing to do." However by beginning with small increments each day, they may discover the joy of a daily walk with Jesus. Daily "lite" can consist of having a Scripture verse on a card nearby or in one's pocket to refer to during the day as a reminder of God's love and presence and reminder to turn to Him in prayer and thanksgiving and when temptations, sinful thoughts, or other challenges arise. The daily card can also be useful for memorizing Scripture, so that when one Scripture has been memorized another can take its place until one has a stack of verses that can be reviewed. One can add additional components, such as daily reading one or more chapters from the Bible. It is important for believers to remember the Lord throughout the day and take brief moments to praise, thank, worship, and adore Him. Numerous Scriptures are helpful reminders, such as Psalm 100. Then as one friend mentioned, he believes that walking according to the Spirit is being 1 John 1:9 up to the nanosecond. By this he means that whenever he catches himself not walking according to the Spirit he confesses his sin and turns back to walking according to the new life Jesus has given him.

Daily "lite" includes some of the basic necessities for nurturing the Spiritual life, but as one grows one will find that "lite" is not enough. As believers mature, they will want the full measure of daily nutrition and will therefore add more time for studying Scripture, praying, and worshipping during a specified time each day. They will also find that they want more of the Lord during the day and will therefore add more times during the day of turning aside in prayer and thanksgiving. They will memorize Scripture to fill their minds with ongoing spiritual nutrition and to be ready with wisdom and truth for the needs of the moment. They will want to utilize the spiritual nutrition through the daily exercise of love, obedience, and service.

46. Be Encouraged to Minister the Life of Christ in You

Person-to person ministry opportunities are everywhere. Throughout this section we have primarily been speaking about ministering to those who seek help for their problems of living, and there are plenty of opportunities there. However, person-to-person ministry is not only for those who seek such help. It is for every believer as various needs arise. This kind of ministry thrives in true Christian fellowship as believers encourage one another in following Christ, and it can occur anywhere from within the family to out in the community, as believers happen to see each other. However, it can also be a very purposeful ministry of reaching out to those in need, such as those suffering the trials of physical illness, those who are infirm and elderly, families that have lost loved ones, young parents who could use a little encouragement and practical help, those who have not yet been incorporated into the life of the church, those who could benefit from personal discipleship, and others who may simply need a ride to church. These are the kinds of person-to-person ministry that are hidden and not broadcast abroad. They do not have the prestige of "counselor," but they are exceedingly pleasing to God. Such person-to-person ministry is the true ministry of mutual care. In fact, if Christians were to purposefully involve themselves in this mutual care there would be few who would seek problem-centered counseling help.

Person-to-person ministry is shared among the body of believers so that the dependency is on Christ in the context of His Body. It should follow the natural function of the body as described in Romans 12 where believers share the joys and sorrows of life with one another. It does not function as an entity unto itself, as so much of the biblical counseling movement does, confined to counseling offices and problem-centered conversations. While the one who ministers can meet someone in a church office, there is no such limitation in person-to-person ministry. The biblical helper may minister to individuals, couples, and families in homes, as well as in a great variety of other places. Furthermore, the relationship of love and care goes beyond conversation when practical assistance is needed, just as James 2:15-16 says:

> If a brother or sister be naked, and destitute of daily food, And one of you say unto them, Depart in peace, be ye warmed and filled; notwithstanding ye give them not those things which are needful to the body; what doth it profit?

And, of course all of this can be shared within the fellowship of believers.

When believers are walking according to the Spirit and seeking to serve the Lord they will find opportunities to minister. In fact, they may find more opportunities than they can fulfill and that is where they can encourage fellow believers to come alongside and join them in mutual care. Churches may develop programs in their attempt to meet various needs, but so often the programs become ends in themselves and the normal spiritual function of Christ's Body becomes replaced by programs. Some form of organization may be necessary to inform believers of needs in the fellowship, such as when there is illness and a family needs meals or when fellow believers are in need of visitation or assistance. On the other hand individual believers often know of needs and may seek the Lord as to whether or how they might minister. Much of this should happen naturally as believers fellowship together and grow in their love for one another and as pastors and leaders teach them about mutual care according to the Word.

As believers move away from talking about problems towards giving attention to Christ and growing into His likeness, there will be evidence of spiritual growth. There will be more of Jesus and less of self. There will be greater love for God and others. Believers will be motivated to walk according to the Spirit rather than the flesh and have an earnest desire to please God. They will grow in humility with a keen understanding of the depravity of their own flesh, which is to be put off and counted dead. As believers become more and more occupied with Christ, they will bear more fruit of the Spirit. Then, instead of needing ministry, they will be able to minister to others.

Ever since the Day of Pentecost there have been believers who have turned to the Lord during trials, and there are still many believers who turn to the Lord and spiritually mature through their suffering. These are living epistles of the work of Christ during difficult circumstances. Throughout the centuries God has used ordinary believers to minister His life through the preaching of the Gospel to unbelievers. He also used ordinary believers to minister His Word and His life to fellow believers long before the intrusion of psychological theories and therapies into the church and long before the contemporary biblical counseling movement. We rejoice that even now such Christ-centered ministry continues quietly as needs arise among believers. These are not the people who would be noticed by the world. They are the saints who are seen by the Lord Himself as they labor quietly behind the scenes to minister the life of Christ to one another. **May more** believers find their freedom in Christ to step out in faith to minister His Word and His Life for salvation of the lost and for the edification of fellow saints who are suffering from problems of living. May they do so by depending on God, His Word, and His ongoing work in each believer.

We Pray!

We pray that as a result of reading this book, biblical counselors and all believers will abandon problem-centered sinful communication, embrace the biblical truths about the role of problems in a believer's life, and become Christ-centered on a daily basis in their own lives and in all they minister to one another.

We pray that the reading of this book and knowing What Not to Do, What to Avoid, and What Can Be Done will give greater courage to those who already minister and to many others whom God has equipped to move forward and to care for souls as He has intended through the Word and the work of the Holy Spirit in the fellowship of the saints.

We pray that this book will be an encouragement for believers to minister in the humility of mutual care and not to consider their own counsel to be the final word.

We pray that others who truly minister biblically will supplement and augment what we have written with what they have found in the vast treasure house of God's Word.

We pray that, if you are born again, maturing in the faith through the trials of life with growing dependency on the Word of God through the work of the Holy Spirit, you will know that you are equipped to minister to others as God has ministered to you.

Finally, our joy over the years has been in those individuals who, wholly without counseling certificates, degrees, manuals, books or programs, have ministered to others entirely unintimidated by lack of counseling education and training, just as the saints in the past have done prior to the rise of the psychological and biblical counseling movements.

We say to all who have been prepared by the Lord: Go and
minister by grace through faith.

Appendix A

Old Testament "Counsel"[1]

In the Old Testament there are just five English words (translated from a number of Hebrew words) that seem to relate to the currently used term *counseling*. They are *counsel, counselled, counsellor, counsellors,* and *counsels.* The words translated as *counsellor* and *counsellors* are used in reference to the person giving the counsel. The other ones have to do with what is counseled.

There are at least two ways to examine these words: in their original meaning and in their context. The most frequently used word and its derivatives can be translated as "advise, counsel, purpose, devise, plan."[2] The repeated usage of the word *counsel* is for decision making or to accomplish a goal. For instance, when Absalom conspired to take the kingdom away from his father and sought counsel, Ahithophel proposed a plan to pursue David, smite him, and then bring those who had followed David back to Absalom. However, when Absalom consulted Hushai about the plan, Hushai said, "The counsel that Ahithophel hath given is not good at this time." Hushai then proposed another plan by which Absalom, instead, would be defeated (2 Samuel 17).

Counsel had to do with plans, guidance, and advice. Psalm 1:1 says, "Blessed is the man that walketh not in the counsel of the ungodly." That is, do not follow the advice, guidance, or plans of the ungodly. Psalm 2:2 gives another example of counsel: "The kings of the earth set themselves, and the rulers take counsel together, against the Lord, and

235

against his anointed." Here a group is devising a plan in opposition to God.

If one compares the actual, contextual use of the word *counsel*, as well as the words *counsels* and *counselled*, one will see a great contrast between the biblical use of those words and the current biblical counselors who counsel people in their daily problems of living, habitual sins, emotional-behavioral problems, or any other such terms one might use. While there may be times when biblical counselors devise plans, propose a course of action, and give advice, the current practice of biblical counseling contains elements that go beyond the biblical use of the word *counsel*.

The most often misused example to establish biblical counseling is found in Exodus 18:13-26. The passage begins with a picture of Moses as he "sat to judge the people" and as "the people stood by Moses from the morning unto the evening." Moses' father-in-law, Jethro, asked Moses why that was happening and Moses answered:

> Because the people come unto me to inquire of God: When they have a matter, they come unto me; and I judge between one and another, and I do make them know the statutes of God, and his laws (Exodus 18:15-16).

In other words, Moses was judging according to the law of God. The word *counsel* is not even used to describe what Moses was doing. The word *counsel* is not used until Jethro is ready to give advice and present a plan to Moses, when Jethro said to Moses: "Hearken now unto my voice, I will give thee counsel." Jethro then presented a plan for Moses to teach the ordinances of God to the people and to:

> . . . provide out of all the people able men, such as fear God, men of truth, hating covetousness; and place such over them, to be rulers of thousands, and

rulers of hundreds, rulers of fifties, and rulers of tens: And let them judge the people at all seasons: and it shall be, that every great matter they shall bring unto thee, but every small matter they shall judge: so shall it be easier for thyself, and they shall bear the burden with thee (Exodus 18:21,22).

One commentary says the following about Moses:

Having been employed to redeem Israel out of the house of bondage, herein he is a further type of Christ, that he is employed as a lawgiver and a judge among them. (1) He was to answer enquiries, and to explain the laws of God that were already given them, concerning the Sabbath, the manna, &c., beside the laws of nature, relating both to piety and equity, *v* 15. Moses made them *know the statutes of God and his laws, v.* 16. His business was, not to make laws, but to make known God's laws; his place was but that of a servant. (2) He was to decide controversies, judging between a man and his fellow, *v* 16. And, if the people were as quarrelsome one with another as they were with God, no doubt he had a great many causes brought before him.[3]

It must also be remembered that this incident preceded Mt. Sinai and the receiving of the Ten Commandments. Moses was judging the people. He was resolving controversies when disagreements occurred. He was not counseling problems of living like a contemporary biblical counselor, but was judging according to the "ordinances and laws." While judging according to the "ordinances and laws" may be included in biblical counseling, there is a great difference between what Moses was doing and what present-day biblical counselors generally do. Examples of some of the differences are given in Part Two, which describes what goes on in problem-centered biblical counseling.

In their eagerness to justify what they do, those who refer to themselves as "biblical counselors" turn judges into counselors who follow a pattern that more resembles psychological counseling than judging by God's laws and ordinances. Many years ago, in our own eagerness for counseling according to the Word of God, we used Jethro's counsel to Moses to encourage pastors to share the burden of personal counsel with members of the body. We continue to believe that the principle of sharing the burden applies, but we now conclude that the story of Jethro's advice to Moses is misapplied as a justification for the methodology of what is currently called "biblical counseling."

Counselors in the church also use Isaiah 9:6 to justify their practice of counseling.

> For unto us a child is born, unto us a son is given: and the government shall be upon his shoulder: and his name shall be called Wonderful, Counsellor, The mighty God, The everlasting Father, The Prince of Peace (Isaiah 9:6).

Isaiah 9:6 prophetically describes the coming Messiah, the Lord Jesus Christ. In this passage Jesus is called "Wonderful, Counsellor." The authorized King James Version separates the words *wonderful* from *counselor* with a comma, but Hebrew scholars say that the word *wonderful* is used to describe *counselor*. Therefore we looked into the meaning of both words. The word *wonderful* is the translation of the Hebrew word *pele'*. The *Theological Wordbook of the Old Testament* defines the Hebrew word *pele'* as "wonder" and says that it is: "Always in a context of God's acts or words, except for Lam 1:9. The root appears most frequently in the Psalms."[4] Thus it has to do with the wonder of the miraculous. It is beyond the common meaning of *wonderful* in English.

The word *counselor* (KJV) is from the Hebrew word *yâ'ats*, which means "advise, counsel, purpose, devise, plan," and is translated by a word from the Greek *boule* family (word group) in the Septuagint (the Greek translation of the Old Testament). Jesus as counselor is unique in that He is the very Word of God who "was made flesh, and dwelt among us" (John 1:14). He did not practice counseling as those who call themselves "biblical counselors" today. There were no ongoing sessions centered around individual people's problems. He knew the heart and spoke forth the Word of Truth. Today we receive His counsel through the written Word together with the Holy Spirit. The involvement of the Holy Spirit in the Lord's counsel can be seen in Isaiah 11:1-2:

> And there shall come forth a rod out of the stem of Jesse, and a Branch shall grow out of his roots: And the spirit of the LORD shall rest upon him, the spirit of wisdom and understanding, the spirit of counsel and might, the spirit of knowledge and of the fear of the LORD.

Jesus is the Branch, and the word translated *counsel* comes from a derivative of the same Hebrew word as translated *counsellor* in Isaiah 9:6. The connection is clearly seen between the Wonderful Counselor and the "spirit of counsel." Therefore, this Hebrew word group cannot be used to justify the kind of counseling that goes on today. Nevertheless, we can be confident that God will continue to give counsel through His Word and His Holy Spirit. That is why solid Bible preaching, teaching, and evangelizing are so vital today and must be an integral part of ministering to individuals, couples, and families in need.

Appendix B

New Testament "Counsel"[1]

In the New Testament, there are three words used in translation that seem to relate to the currently used terms in counseling. They are *counsel*, *counsellor*, and *counsels*. One of these words (*counsellor*) has to do with the person or persons giving the counsel. The remaining two have to do with what is counseled. Nevertheless, there is no example of biblical counseling as it is practiced in the church today. The English word *counsel* is used 19 times in the New Testament (KJV, Strong's *Concordance*[1]) and each comes from the Greek *boule* word group, which means purpose, will, decision, resolution, counsel, or advice. If one looks under the word *counsel* in a concordance and then reads this New Testament word in the context of the verses listed, it will hardly be necessary to look in the Greek dictionary to understand the meaning.

In many instances the word *counsel* is used to describe the actions of those who opposed Jesus and His disciples. For instance, Matthew 27:1 says, "When the morning was come, all the chief priests and elders of the people took counsel together against Jesus to put him to death." The word translated *counsel* in that and similar passages refers to the idea of consulting together.

In contrast to the wicked counsel engaged in by the enemies of Christ is the counsel of God, such as in Ephesians 1:11, which speaks of believers "being predestinated according to the purpose of him who worketh all things after

241

the counsel of his own will." The same word is used in Acts 20:27, when Paul says, "For I have not shunned to declare unto you all the counsel of God." Indeed some biblical counselors will declare much counsel of God in the process of their counseling, and that is what should go on in ministries among believers. Yet, again, that is only part of what occurs in contemporary biblical counseling. The contemporary use of *counsel* in reference to biblical counseling relates only distantly and tangentially to the meanings of the words used in the New Testament.

The word *counsellor* is used three times in the New Testament. Two of the times are used to describe Joseph of Arimathaea and refer to his position as a member of the Jewish Sanhedrin. The other verse is Romans 11:34: "For who hath known the mind of the Lord? or who hath been his counsellor?" In other words, who would be so arrogant as to think he could advise God?

The only other word used is *counsels*, which is used only once, in 1 Corinthians 4:5: "Therefore judge nothing before the time, until the Lord come, who both will bring to light the hidden things of darkness, and will make manifest the counsels of the hearts: and then shall every man have praise of God." It is simply the plural of *boule*, which means purpose, will, decision, resolution, counsel, or advice. In this context *counsels* would refer to inner advising, planning, and directing within the heart of man.

Obviously the New Testament use of the words translated as *counsel*, *counsellor*, and *counsels* do have shades of meaning in the Greek. However, in no instance does the use of those words justify what is currently called "biblical counseling" in the twenty-first century. We are not saying that these are the only words and examples associated with counseling in the Old and New Testaments. What we are saying is that there is no counseling with its roles of counselor and counselee found in the Bible as presently conducted by those who call themselves biblical counselors. One cannot use the biblical meaning of the above words to defend the practice of contemporary biblical counseling. These terms have been usurped from secular use, retrofitted to Scripture, and then rationalized to be biblical.

One of the root meanings of the Greek words *sumboulos* and *bouleutes* translated *counsellor* or *counselor* is adviser. If contemporary counselors, such as those in the BCM, functioned as in the Bible, a person or couple would come seeking advice. The advice would be given and that would be the end of it. There would not be a need for continually discussing and convincing followed by a number of problem-centered sessions as with the BCM.

Christ-centered ministry focuses on building one's faith through truth (see Part Three) to encourage the troubled individual to grow spiritually, mature in the faith, and deal with his/her own problems as others do in relationship with the Lord. When one compares how Jesus and Paul ministered with the way those in the BCM counsel, there is a dramatic difference. While they may do some similar things as Jesus and Paul did, those in the BCM counsel more like secular counselors than like Jesus and Paul.

End Notes

What This Book Is All About

1   The Greek word translated "evil speaking" in Ephesians 4:31 is also translated "blasphemy." Regarding the word *blasphemy*, Davis says: "In general the word means simply slander or insult and includes any action (e.g., a gesture) as well as any word that devalues another person or being, living or dead.... In the NT blasphemy occurs in its wider Greek meaning as well as its specifically religious sense, for people are slandered, not just God (Rom. 3:8; 1 Cor. 10:30; Eph. 4:31; Titus 3:2)." Peter H. Davids, "Blasphemy," *Evangelical Dictionary of Theology*, 2nd ed., Walter A. Elwell, ed. Grand Rapids, MI: Baker Academic, 1984, p 174.

Part One: What Not to Do

1   See Martin and Deidre Bobgan. *PsychoHeresy: The Psychological Seduction of Christianity* (1987); *The End of "Christian Psychology"* (1997); and *Against "Biblical Counseling": For the Bible* (1994); *Christ-Centered Ministry versus Problem-Centered Counseling* (2004) [Santa Barbara, CA: East-Gate Publishers]; articles from *PsychoHeresy Awareness Letter* articles now posted on www.psychoheresy-aware.org.

2   Bobgan and Bobgan, *Christ-Centered Ministry versus Problem-Centered Counseling, op. cit.*, p. 9.

3   *Ibid.*, p. 17.

4   Jay E. Adams. *Update on Christian Counseling*, Vol. 1 and 2. Grand Rapids: Zondervan, 1977, 1979, 1981, Introduction to Vol. 2.

5   Bobgan and Bobgan, *Against "Biblical Counseling": For the Bible, op. cit.*, pp. 73ff.

6   Bobgan and Bobgan, *PsychoHeresy, op. cit.*

7   Ellen Herman. *The Romance of American Psychology: Political Culture in the Age of Experts*. Berkeley: University of California Press, 1996, p. 1.

8   John T. McNeill. *A History of The Cure of Souls*. New York; Harper & Row, Publishers, 1951, p. vii.

9   Thomas Szasz. *The Myth of Psychotherapy*. Garden City: Doubleday/Anchor Press, 1978, p. 25.

10   *Ibid.*, p. 26.

11   Robert C. Fuller. *Mesmerism and the American Cure of Souls*. Philadelphia: University of Pennsylvania Press, 1982, p. xii.

12   Szasz, *op. cit.*, p. 25.

13 *Ibid.*, p. xxiv.

14 *Ibid.*, p. 8.

15 *Ibid.*, p. 11.

16 Rogers H. Wright and Nicholas A. Cummings, eds. *The Practice of Psychology: The Battle for Professionalism.* Phoenix AZ: Zeig, Tucker & Theisen, Inc., 2001, p. 2.

17 *Ibid.*, p. 3.

18 Herman, *op. cit.*, p. 3.

19 *Ibid.*, p. 5.

20 Herman, *op. cit.*, p. 275.

21 *Ibid.*, p. 311.

22 Bernie Zilbergeld. *The Shrinking of America.* Boston: Little, Brown and Company, 1983, p. 11.

23 Janice Peck. *The Age of Oprah.* Boulder, CO: Paradigm Publishers, 2008, p. 5.

24 See Bobgan and Bobgan, *Against "Biblical Counseling": For the Bible* and *Christ-Centered Ministry versus Problem-Centered Counseling, op. cit.*

25 "Counseling Encourages Talebearing," *PsychoHeresy Awareness Letter*, May-June, 2005, http://www.psychoheresy-aware.org/talebearing.html.

26 Jay Lebow. "War of the Worlds: Researchers and Practitioners Collide on EMDR and CISD." *Psychotherapy Networker*, Vol. 27, No. 5, p. 79.

27 See Bobgan and Bobgan, *Against "Biblical Counseling": For the Bible* and *Christ-Centered Ministry versus Problem-Centered Counseling, op. cit.*

28 Carol Tavris and Elliot Aronson. *Mistakes Were Made (but not by me).* New York: Harcourt, Inc., 2007.

29 "Born Again Adults Less Likely to Co-Habit, Just as Likely to Divorce." Barna Research Online, August 6, 2001, www.barna.org.

30 Richard Simon. "From the Editor." *Psychotherapy Networker*, Vol. 26, No. 6, p. 2.

31 Stuart Scott, Plenary Speaker, NANC national meeting, Little Rock, AR, October 5-7, 1998.

32 David Powlison, "Idols of the Heart and 'Vanity Fair,'" *The Journal of Biblical Counseling*, Winter 1995, pp. 35ff.

33 Bobgan and Bobgan, *Against "Biblical Counseling": For the Bible, op. cit.*, pp. 57-72.

34 Jay E. Adams, "What is Biblical Counseling?" www.gateway-biblical-counseling.net/definition.html.

35 Jay E. Adams. *The Christian Counselor's New Testament.* Grand Rapids, MI: Baker Book House, 1977, 1980.

36 W. E. Vine. *The Expanded Vine's Expository Dictionary of New Testament Words*, John R. Kohlenberger III, ed. Minneapolis: Bethany House, 1984; Walter Bauer. *A Greek-English Lexicon of the New Testament and Other Early Christian Literature*, translated and adapted by William F. Arndt and F. Wilbur Gingrich, Second Edition revised and augmented by F. Wilbur Gin-

grich and Frederick W. Danker. Chicago: The University of Chicago Press, 1957, 1979.

37 Jay E. Adams, "What is Biblical Counseling?" *op. cit.*

38 Charles J. Sykes. *A Nation of Victims.* New York: St. Martin's Press, 1992, p. 11.

39 *Ibid.*, pp. 14-15.

40 *Ibid.*, p. 15.

41 Louann Brizendine. *The Female Brain.* New York: Morgan Road Books, 2006, inside jacket cover.

42 "Sex Differences," *Wikipedia.*

43 Carl Sherman, "Man's Last Stand: What Does It Take to Get a Guy into Therapy?" *Psychology Today*, Vol. 37, No. 4, p. 71.

44 Terrence Real, quoted by Sherman, *ibid.*

45 Gary R. Brooks. *A New Psychotherapy for Traditional Men.* San Francisco: Jossey-Bass Publishers, 1998, pp. 41-42.

46 Martin and Deidre Bobgan. *Missions & PsychoHeresy.* Santa Barbara, CA: EastGate Publishers, 2000.

47 Carol Tharp, M.D., personal letter.

48 Bobgan and Bobgan, *Against "Biblical Counseling": For the Bible, op. cit.*, Chapters 4 and 5.

49 Such as Larry Crabb, James Dobson. See Bobgan and Bobgan, *Psychoheresy, op. cit.*, Chapter 5.

50 Bobgan and Bobgan, *Against "Biblical Counseling": For the Bible, op. cit.*, pp. 99ff.

51 *Ibid.*, Chapter 3.

52 Martin and Deidre Bobgan, "Pay for Prophecy?" www.psychohersy-aware. org/payproph72.html; "Biblical Counseling: Simoniacs and Pharisaics?" www.psychoheresy-aware.org/bcsimony.html; "NANC & the APA," www. psychoheresy-aware.org/nancap65.html; "$$Simony & Biblical Counseling," www.psychoheresy-aware.org/simonybc.html; "Charging for Biblical Counseling," www.psychoheresy-aware.org/charge75/html; "Shut Down the 'Biblical Counseling' Movement?" www.psychoheresy-aware.org/shutdown. html.

53 *Webster's Encyclopedic Unabridged Dictionary of the English Language.* New York: Gramercy Books, 1996, p. 906.

54 Vine, *The Expanded Vine's Expository Dictionary of New Testament Words, op. cit.*, pp. 551-552.

55 "Controversy Surrounds Bishop Bernard Jordan's New York Ministry," *Charisma*, November 1998, pp. 33-34.

56 *Webster's, op. cit.*, p. 386.

57 *Ibid.*, p. 1544.

58 "$$Simony & Biblical Counseling," *op. cit.*

59 Deborah J. Dewart, "Charging Fees for Biblical Counseling? Relationship, Responsibility, and Remuneration," www.christiandiscernment.com.

Part Two: What to Avoid

1   Jay E. Adams. *Grist from Adams' Mill*. Phillipsburg, NJ: Presbyterian and Reformed Publishing Co., 1983, p. 69.

2   Elizabeth F. Loftus and Melvin J. Guyer. "Who Abused Jane Doe? The Hazards of the Single Case History," Part 1. *Skeptical Inquirer*, Vol. 26, No. 3, p. 24.

3   *Ibid.*, p. 25.

4   Paul E. Meehl. *Psychodiagnosis: Selected Papers*. Minneapolis: University of Minnesota Press, 1973.

5   See Part One, "Counselor, Counselee, Counseling."

6   *Ibid.*

7   Jay E. Adams. *The Case of the "Hopeless Marriage": A Nouthetic Counseling Case from Beginning to End*. Stanley, NC: Timeless Texts, 2006. Subsequent references appear in the text with page numbers.

8   See Part One, "Men in Problem-Centered Counseling."

9   See Part One, "Women in Problem-Centered Counseling."

10 Louann Brizendine. *The Female Brain*. New York: Morgan Road Books, 2006, book jacket.

11 See Part One, "Onerous Ones."

12 See Part One, "Problem-Centered Counseling."

13 Jay E. Adams. *Competent to Counsel*. Grand Rapids, MI: Baker Book House, 1970, p. 93.

14 Jay E. Adams. *The Christian Counselor's Manual*. Grand Rapids, MI: Baker Book House, 1973, p. 187.

15 See Part One, "Marriage Counseling" and "Discussing Marital Problems."

16 See Part One, "Men in Problem-Centered Counseling" and "Women in Problem-Centered Counseling."

17 James Dobson, "Husband Who Feels Suffocated Needs To Be Set Free," *Spartanburg Herald-Journal*, Aug. 26, 1998. Online at http://www.uexpress.com/focusonthefamily/index.html?uc_full_date+20011111.

18 http://www.troubledwith.com

19 Martin and Deidre Bobgan. *James Dobson's Gospel of Self-Esteem & Psychology*. Santa Barbara, CA: EastGate Publishers, 1998.

20 Jay E. Adams. *Growing By Grace*. Stanley, NC: Timeless Texts, 2003, p. 49.

21 http://www.biblicalcounselingcenter.org.

22 David Powlison, "Idols of the Heart and 'Vanity Fair.'" *The Journal of Biblical Counseling*, Vol. 13, No. 2, Winter 1995, pp. 35-50. Subsequent references appear in the text with page numbers.

23 David Powlison, "Crucial Issues in Contemporary Biblical Counseling." *Journal of Pastoral Practice*, Vol. 9, No. 3, 1988, p. 76.

24 Ibid., p. 77.

25 James Strong. *The Exhaustive Concordance of the Bible*. New York: Abingdon Press, 1890, 1894, 1967, pp. 506-507 (word references 1494, 1497).

26 Thomas Szasz. *The Myth of Psychotherapy*. Garden City: Anchor/Double-day, 1978, p. 28.

27 Raymond J. Corsini and Alan J. Auerbach, eds. *Concise Encyclopedia of Psychology*. New York: John Wiley & Sons, Inc., 1996, 1998, p. 306.

28 Ibid., p. 307.

29 Matthew Poole. *A Commentary on the Holy Bible, Vol. II: Psalms-Malachi* (1840). Peabody, MA: Hendrickson Publishers, Inc., 2008 printing, p. 698.

30 Charles J. Sykes. *A Nation of Victims: The Decay of the American Character*. New York: St. Martin's Press, 1992, p. 34.

31 E. Brooks Holifield. *A History of Pastoral Care In America: From Salvation to Self-Realization*. Nashville: Abingdon Press, 1983, p. 23.

32 Tana Dineen. *Manufacturing Victims*. Montreal, Canada: Robert Davies Publishing, 1996.

33 http://www.ccef.org.

34 Martin and Deidre Bobgan. *Against "Biblical Counseling": For the Bible*. Santa Barbara. CA: EastGate Publishers, 1994, pp. 104-105.

35 "AACC & CCEF", http://pamweb.org/aacc_nanc.html.

36 Bobgan, *Against "Biblical Counseling": For the Bible, op. cit.,* pp. 106-108.

37 Martin Bobgan, "Dr. Eric L. Johnson," http://www.psychoheresy-aware.org/eric_johnson.html

38 http://www.ccef.org/counseling_rates.asp.

39 See Part One, "Charging Fees."

40 See Part One, "Problem-Centered Counseling."

41 Letter on file.

42 Martin and Deidre Bobgan. *Against "Biblical Counseling": For the Bible, op. cit.,* p. 11.

43 See Part One, "One-Up/One-Down."

Part Three: What Can Be Done

1 W. E. Vine. *The Expanded Vine's Expository Dictionary of New Testament Words*. Minneapolis: Bethany House Publishers, 1984, p. 199.

Appendix A

1 All biblical references in this section are from the Authorized King James translation.

2 *The Words of the Old Testament*, Vol. 1. R. Laird Harris et al, eds. Chicago: Moody, 1980, p. 390.

3 *Matthew Henry's Commentary in One Volume*. Grand Rapids: Regency Reference Library, Zondervan Publishing House, 1960, p. 91.

4 R. Laird Harris, Gleason L. Archer, Jr., Bruce Waltke. *Theological Word Book of the Old Testament*. Chicago: Moody Press, 1980, Vol. 1, p. 723.

Appendix B

1 James Strong. *The Exhaustive Concordance*. New York: Abingdon Press, 1894, 1967.

Books by Martin & Deidre Bobgan
are also available as free ebooks at:
www.psychoheresy-aware.org

PsychoHeresy: The Psychological Seduction of

Christianity exposes fallacies and failures of psychological counseling theories and therapies. Reveals anti-Christian biases, internal contradictions, and documented failures of secular psychotherapy; and examines amalgamations with Christianity and explodes firmly entrenched myths that undergird these unholy unions.

The End of "Christian Psychology"

describes and analyzes major psychological theories influencing Christians; shows that professional psychotherapy with its underlying psychologies is questionable at best, detrimental at worst, and a spiritual counterfeit at least; and challenges the church to rid itself of all signs and symptoms of this scourge.

Competent to Minister: The Biblical Care of Souls

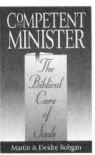

calls Christians back to the Bible and mutual care in the Body of Christ, encourages personal ministry among Christians, and equips believers to minister God's grace through biblical conversation, prayer, and practical help.

The Following Books by Martin & Deidre Bobgan are also available as free ebooks at:
www.psychoheresy-aware.org

12 Steps to Destruction: Codependency/Recovery

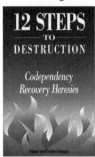

Heresies examines codependency/recovery teachings, Alcoholics Anonymous, twelve-step groups, and addiction treatment programs from a biblical, historical, and research perspective and urges believers to trust in the sufficiency of Christ and the Word of God.

Four Temperaments, Astrology & Personality Testing

examines personality types and tests from a biblical, historical, and research basis and answers such questions as: Do the four temerpaments give true insight into people? Are personality inventories and tests valid ways of finding out about people? What are their occult roots?

Larry Crabb's Gospel

traces Crabb's long journey of jolts, shifts, and expansions as he has sought to create the best combination of psychology and the Bible. Crabb's eclectic theories and methods remain psychologically bound and consistent with current psychotherapy trends. This book provides a detailed analysis.

Christ-Centered Ministry versus Problem-Centered

Counseling is a radical proposal to free believers to minister to one another through Christ-Centered ministry, which empahsizes Christ and His work in the believer through the Word of God, the work of the Holy Spirit, and mutual care in the Body of Christ, without intimidation from the problem-centered psychological and biblical counseling movments.

El ministerio centrado en Cristo comparado con el asesoramiento centrado en el problema is the Spanish translation of *Christ-Centered Ministry versus Problem-Centered Counseling* by the Bobgans.

Hypnosis: Medical, Scientific or Occultic?

examines hypnosis from scientific, historical, and biblical perspectives and shows that hypnosis is the same whether practiced by benevolent medical doctors, shamans, or occultists. The book exposes both obvious and hidden dangers.

James Dobson's Gospel of Self-Esteem & Psychology

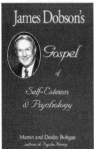

demonstrates that many of Dobson's teachings are based on godless, secular opinions. Self-esteem and psychology are the two major thrusts of his ministry that supercede sin, salvation, and sanctification. They are another gospel.

Against "Biblical Counseling" For the Bible reveals what biblical counseling is, rather than what it pretends or hopes to be. Its primary thrust is to call Christians back to the Bible and to biblically ordained ministries and mutual care in the Body of Christ.

Missions & PsychoHeresy exposes the mental health profession's false façade of expertise for screening missionary candidates and caring for missionaries.It explodes myths about psychological testing and reveals the prolific practice of using mental health professionals to care for missionaries suffering from problems of living.

Theophostic Counseling ~ Divine Revelation? or PsychoHeresy? examines a recovered memory therapy comprised of many existent psychological therapies and techniques, demon deliverance teachings, and elements from the inner healing movement, which include guided imagery, visualization, and hypnosis.

CRI Guilty of PsychoHeresy? answers the CRI-Passantino "Psychology & the Church" series, exposes their illogical reasoning, and argues that supporting psychotherapy and its underlying psychologies is a disgraceful danger in the church.

For a sample copy of *PsychoHeresy Awareness Letter*, a free bimonthly newsletter about the intrusion of psychological counseling theories and therapies into the church, please write to:

PsychoHeresy Awareness Ministries
4137 Primavera Road
Santa Barbara, CA 93110

or call:

1-800-216-4696

<u>www.psychoheresy-aware.org</u>